# The Ultimate Colouring Book Of Birds

## Relax and Unwind

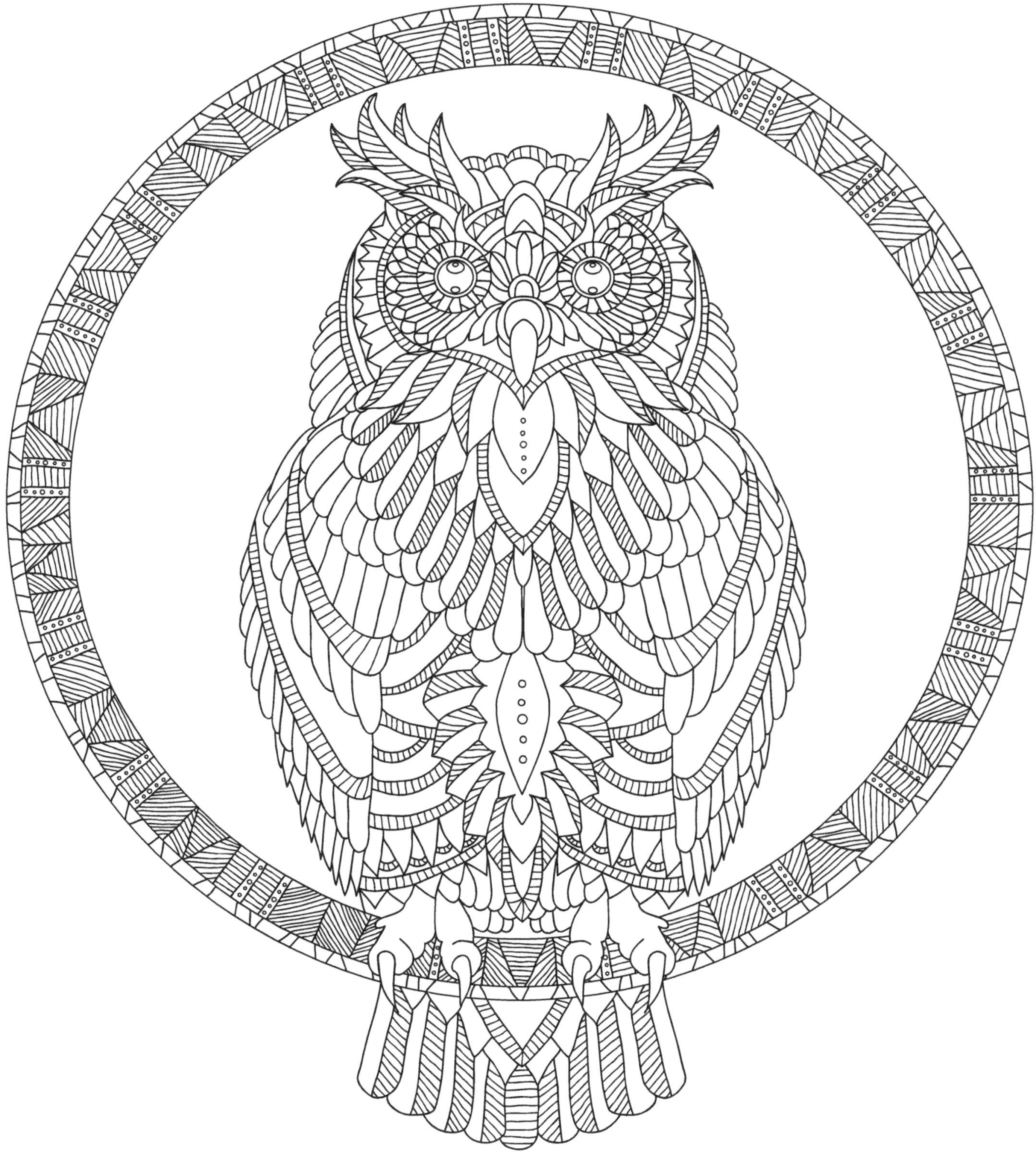

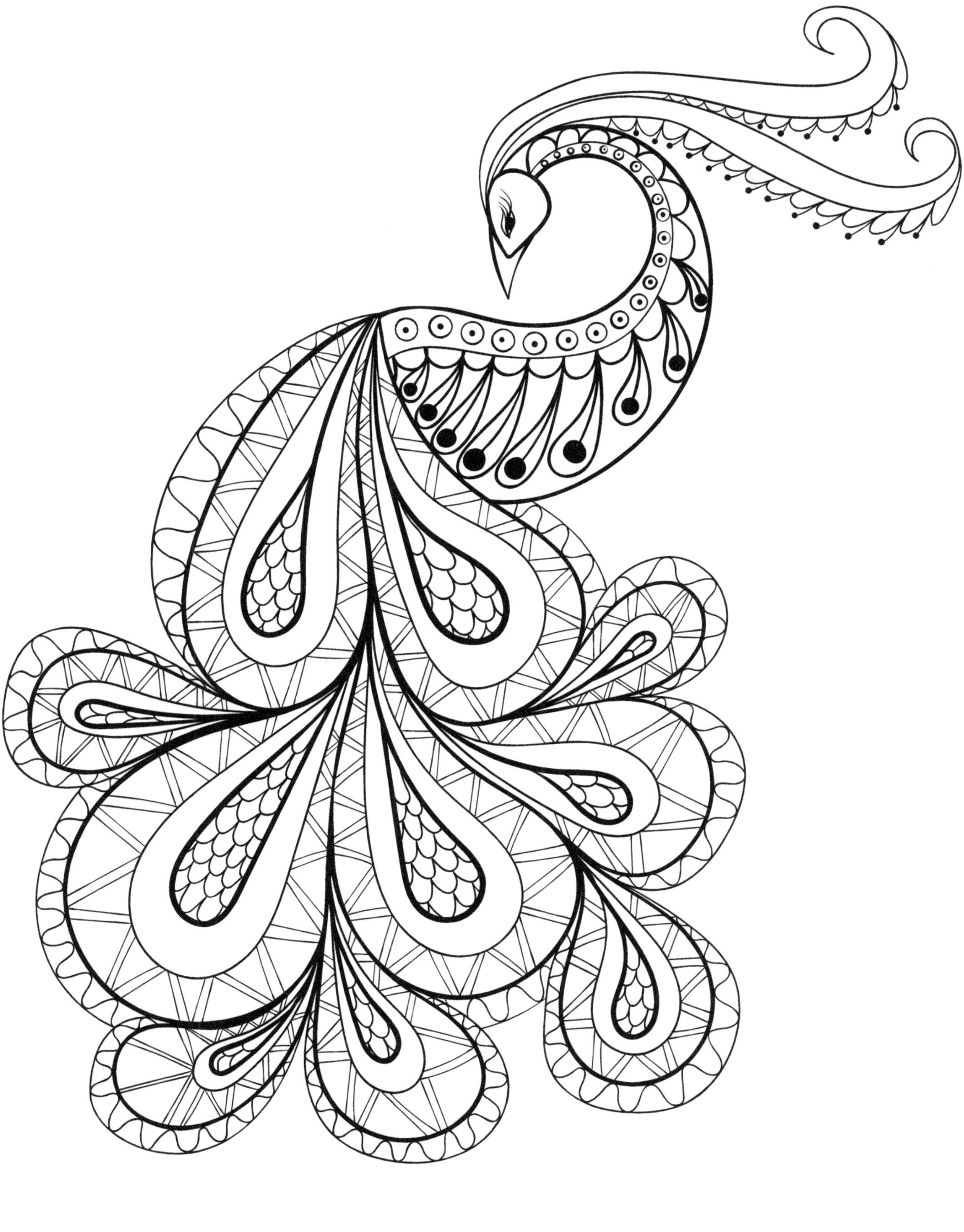

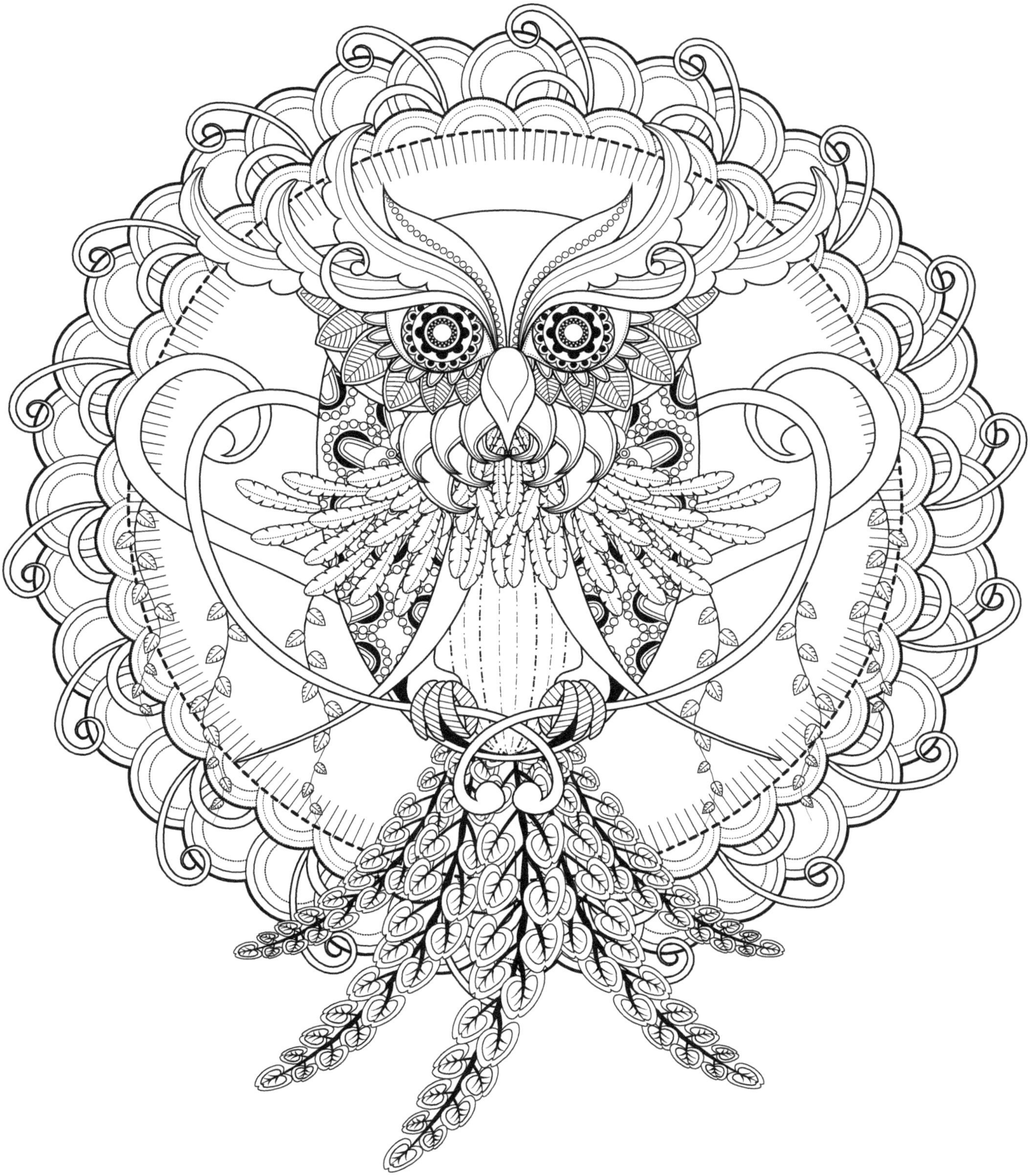

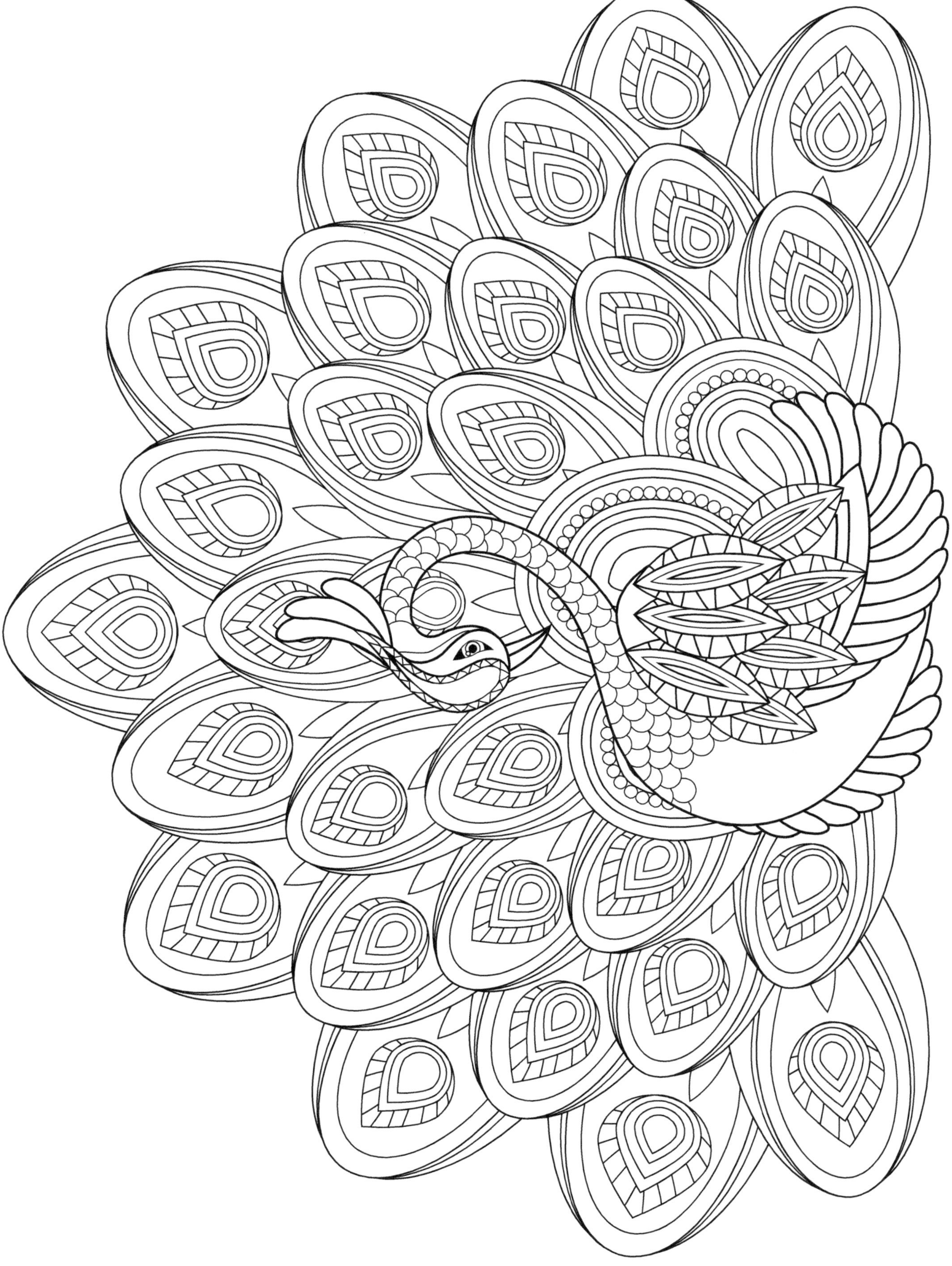

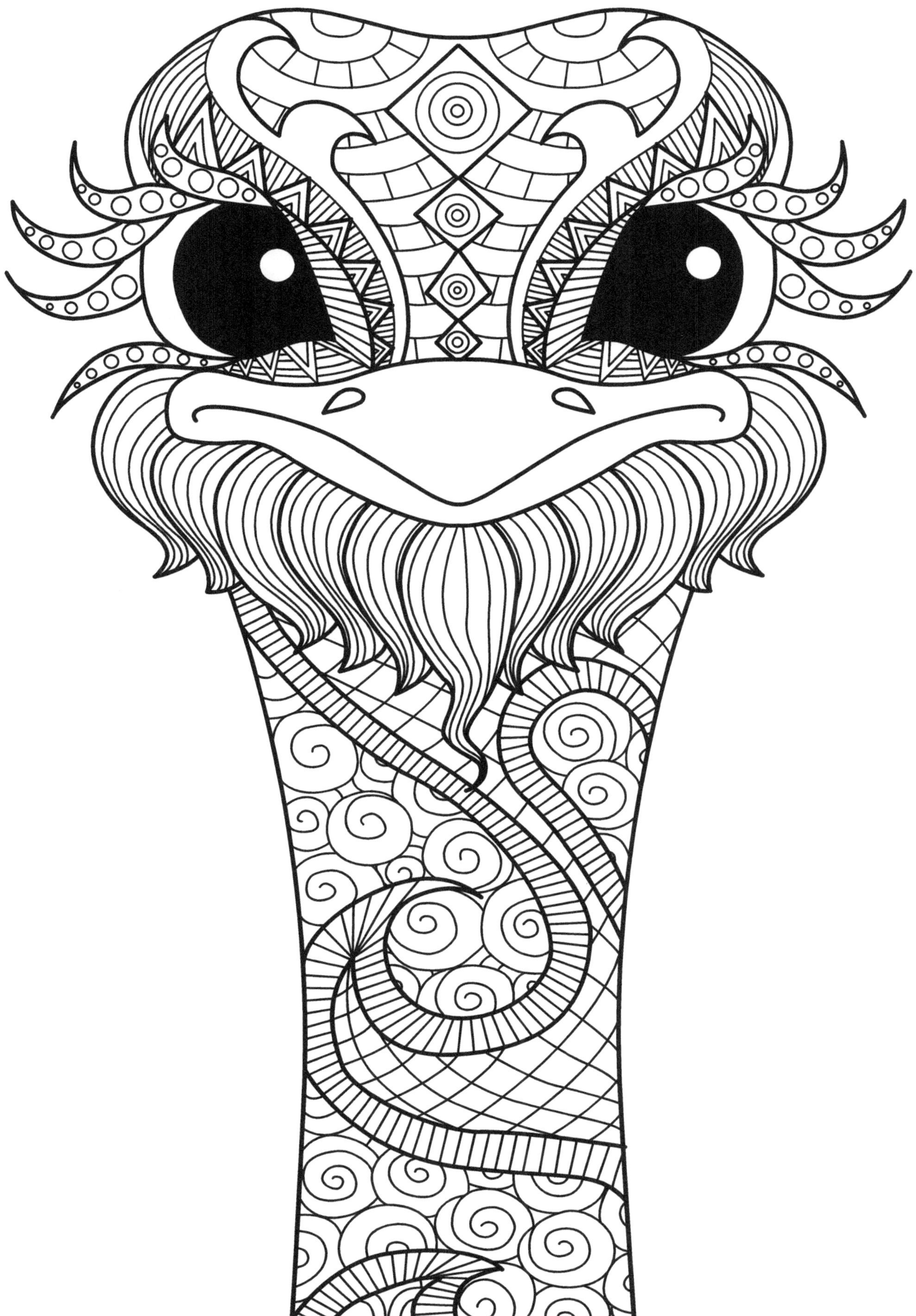

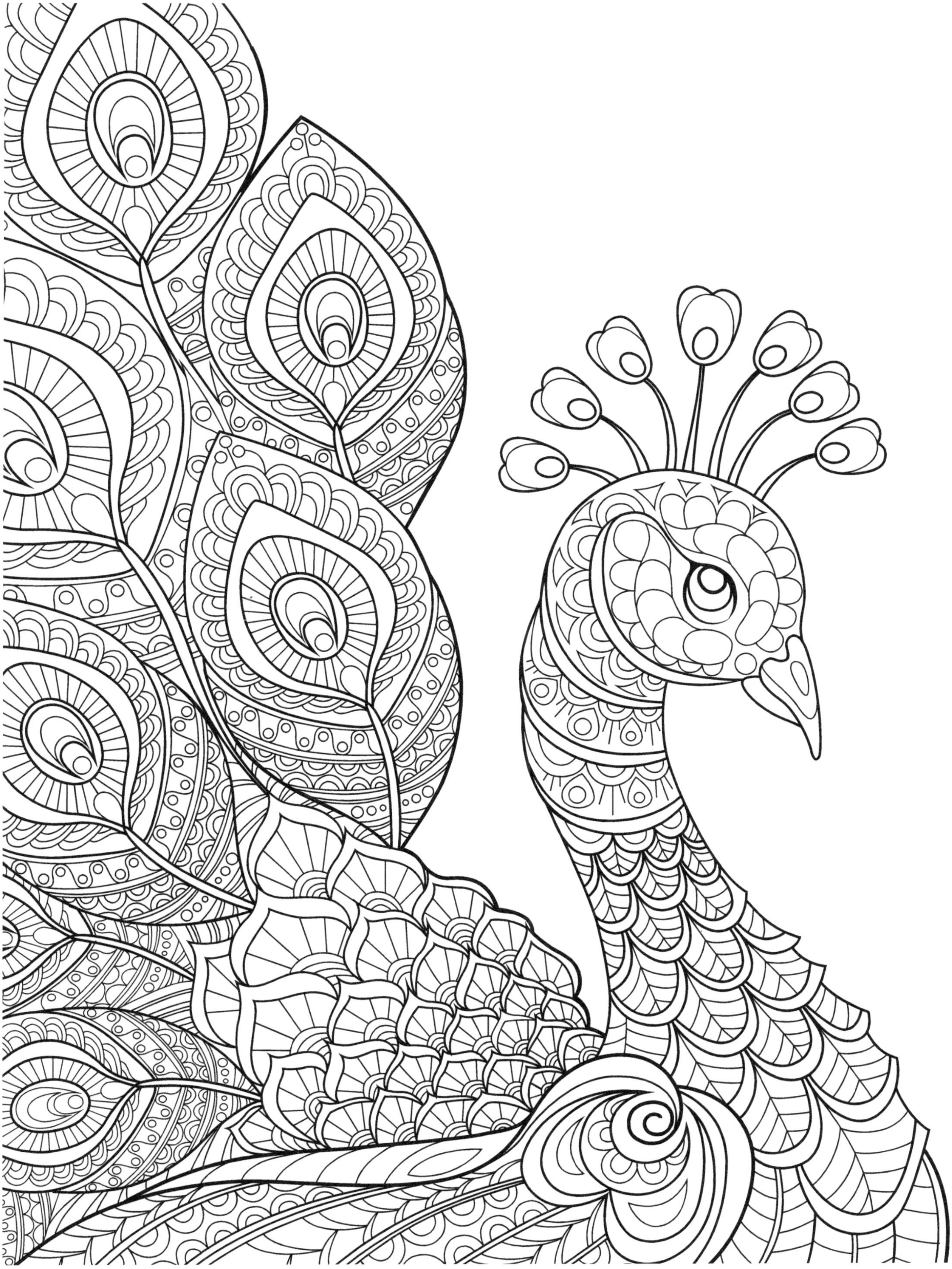

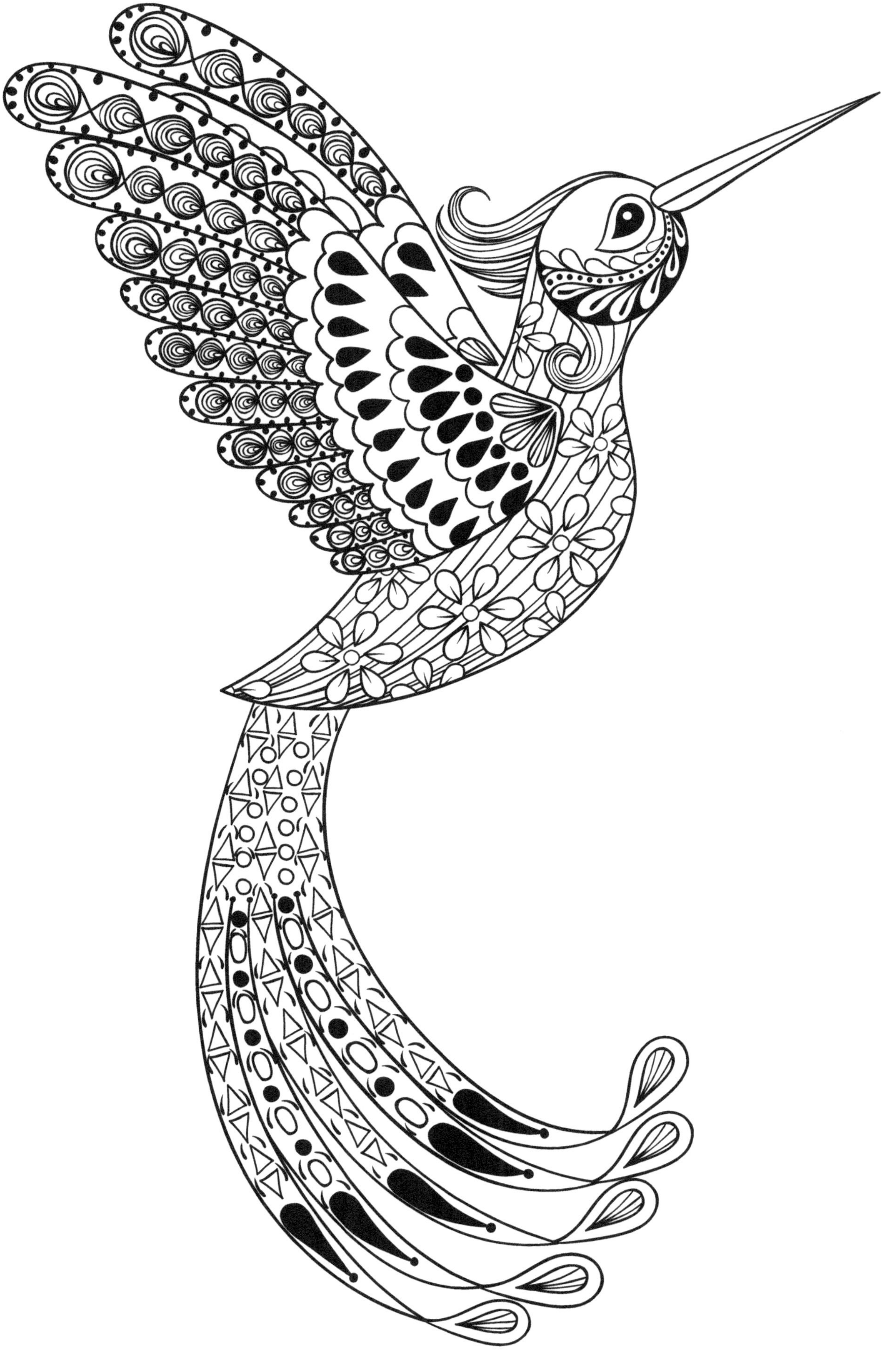

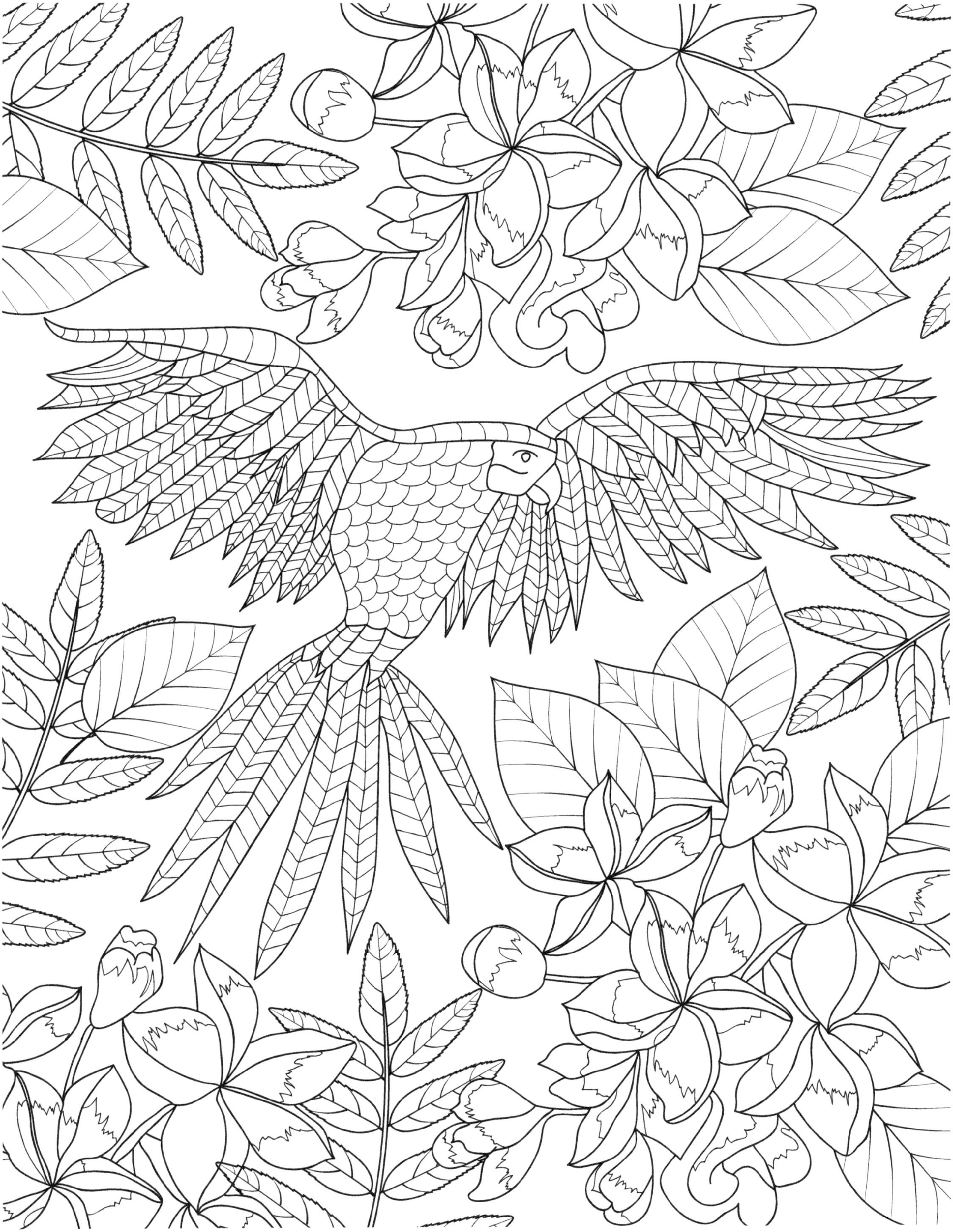

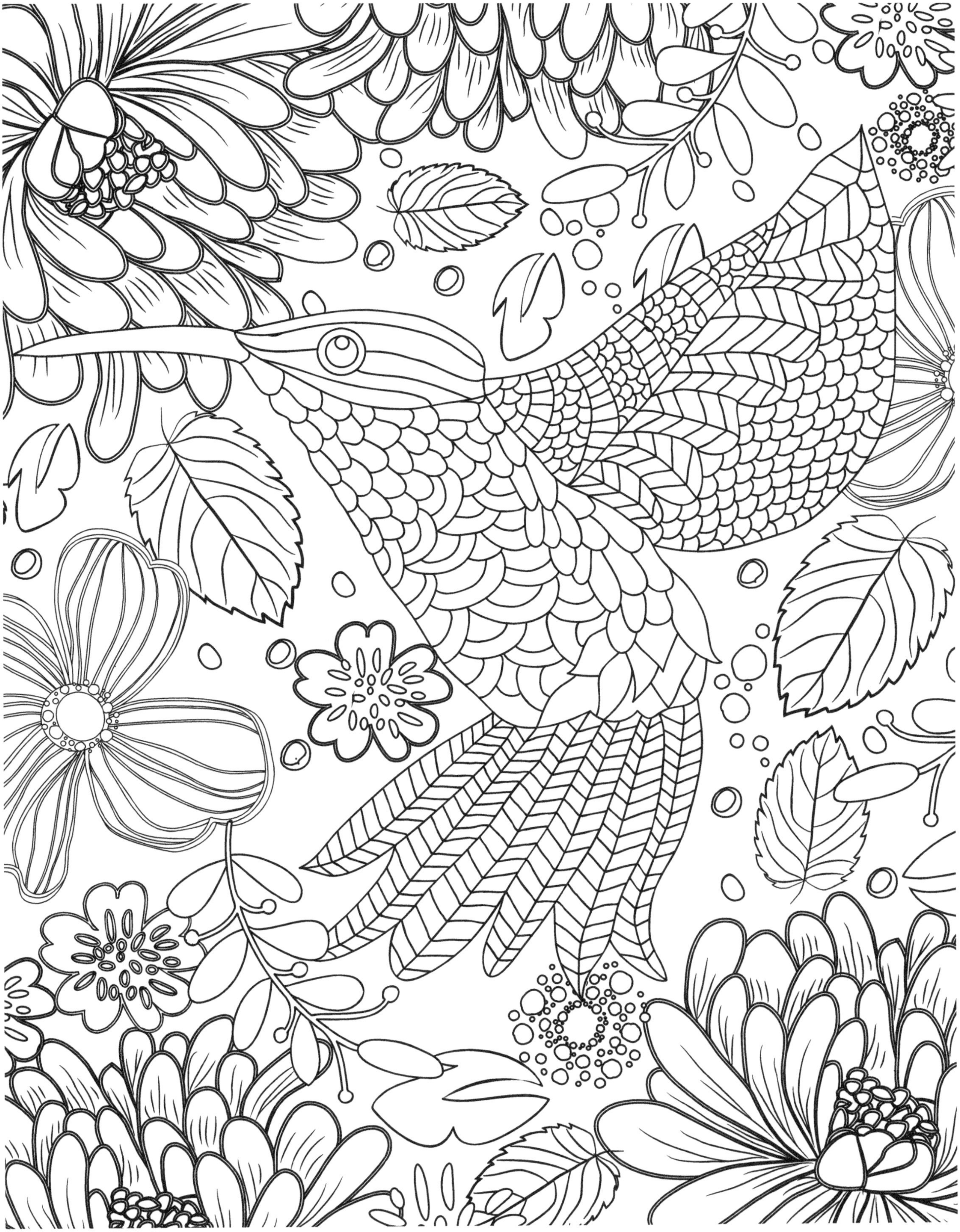

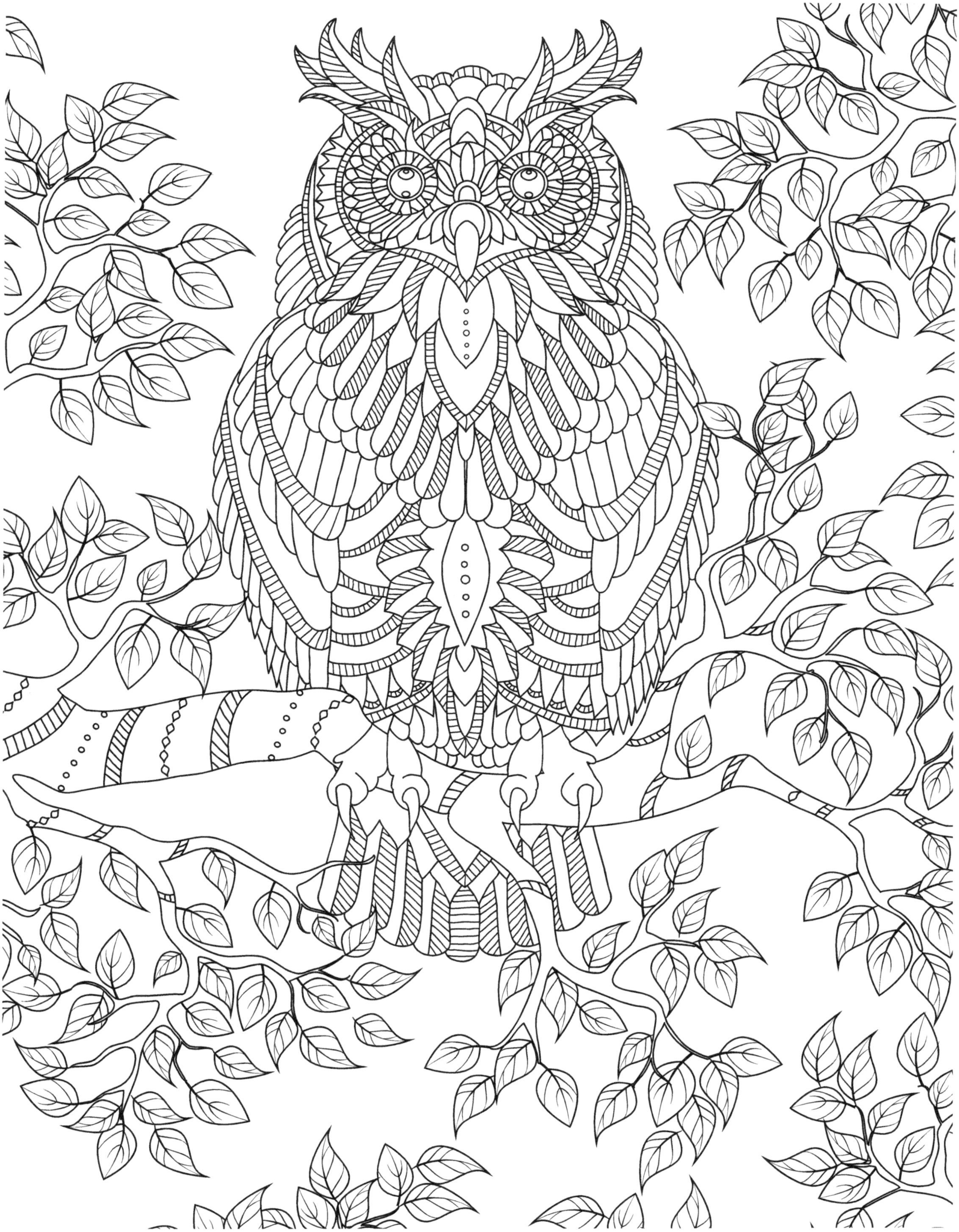

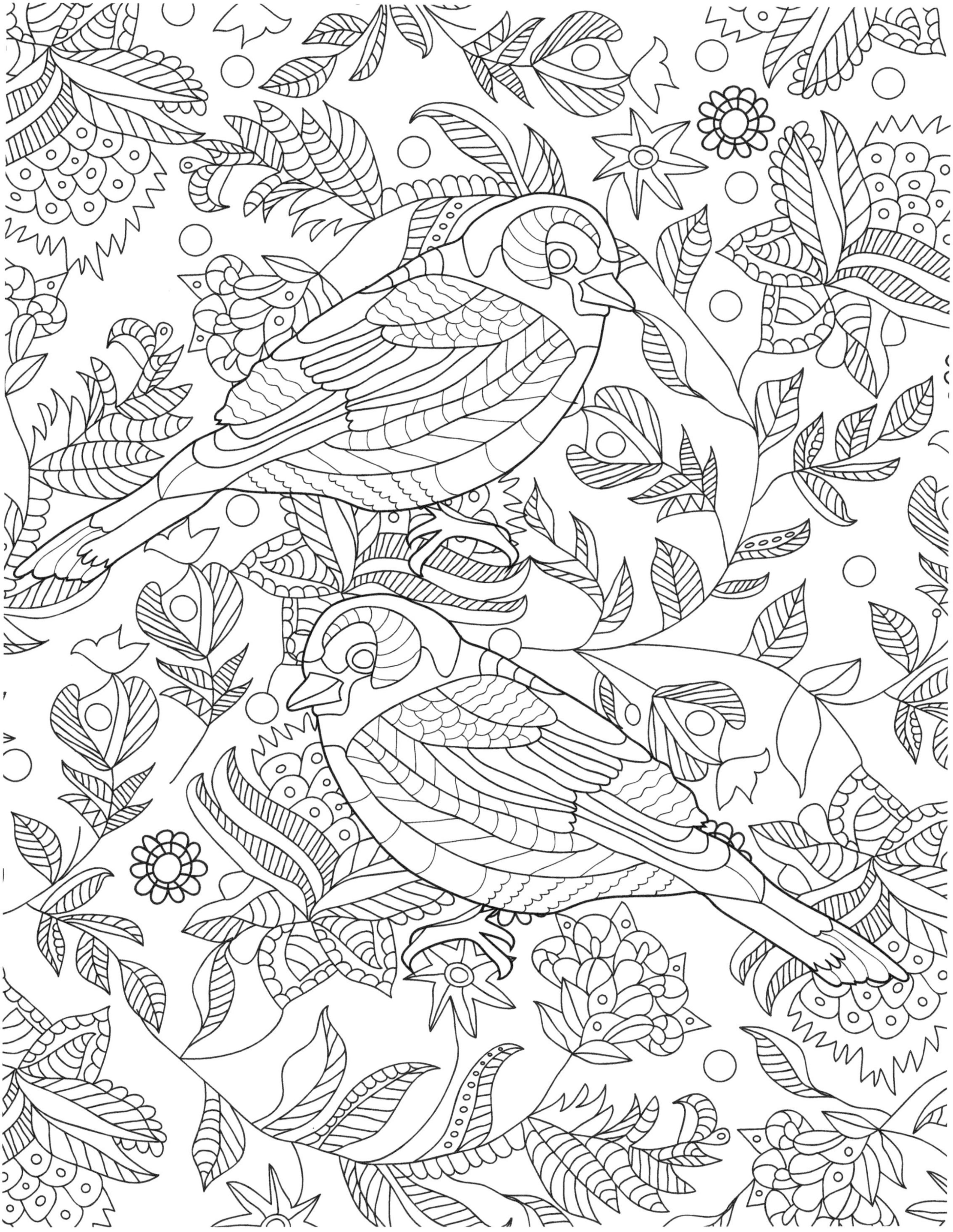

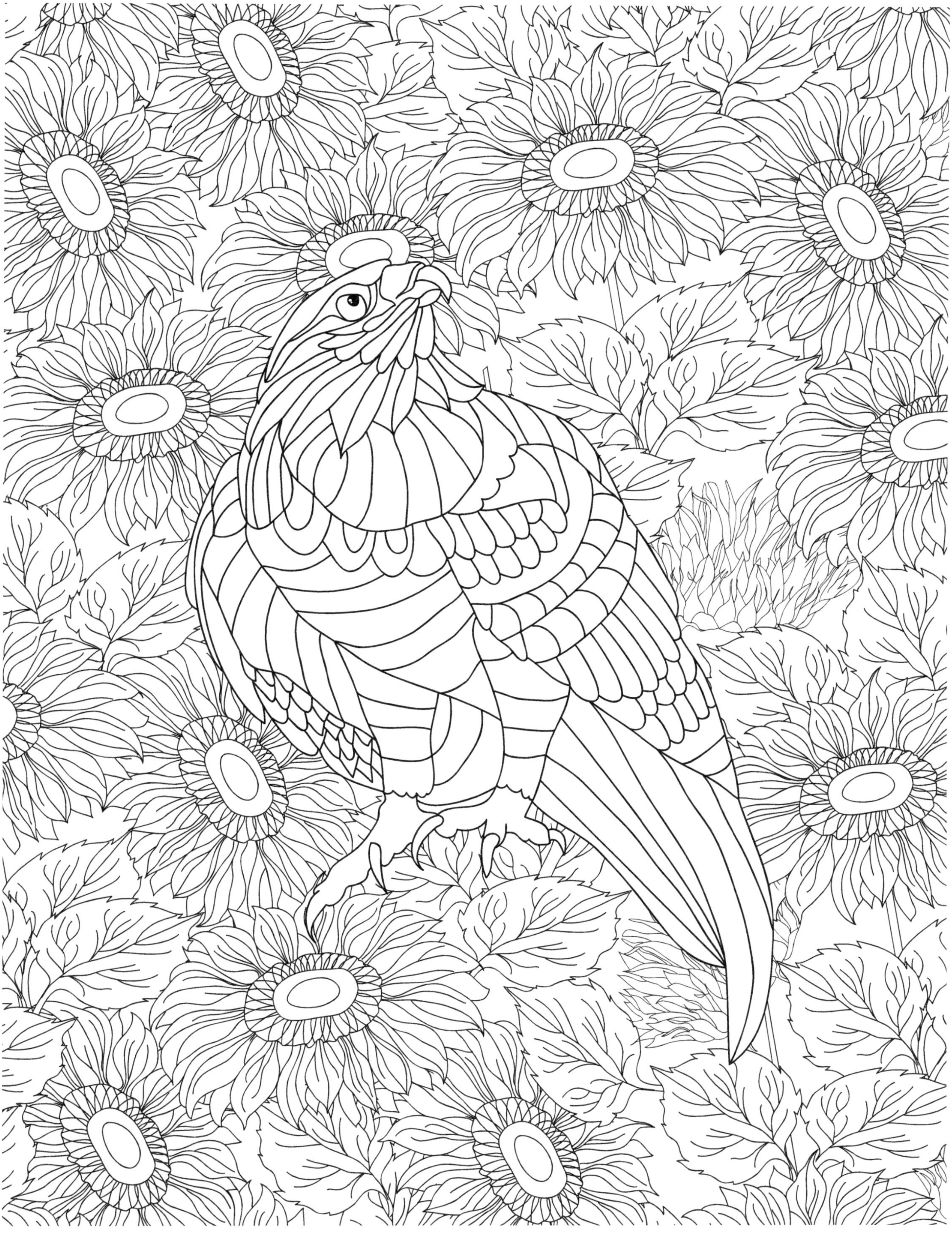

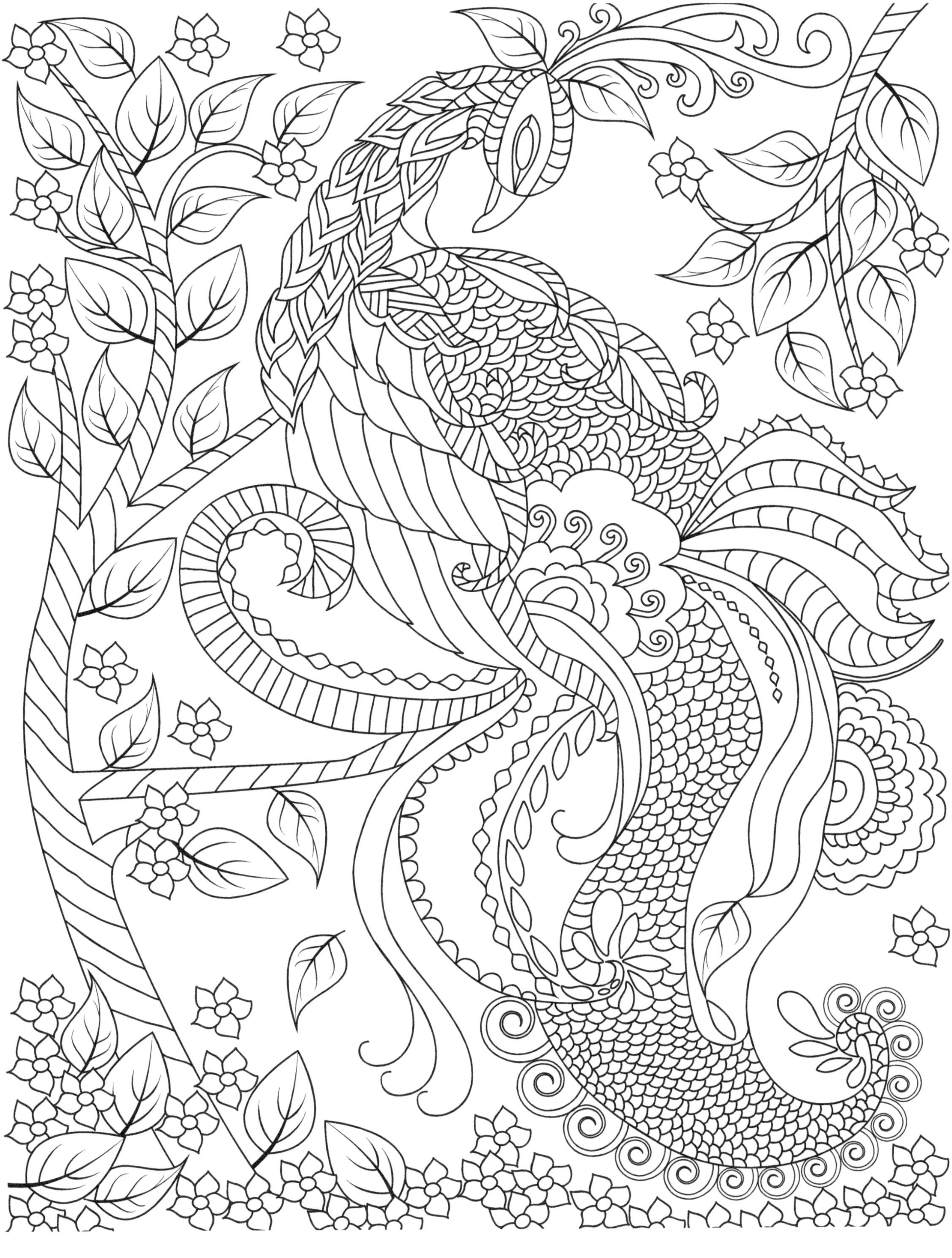

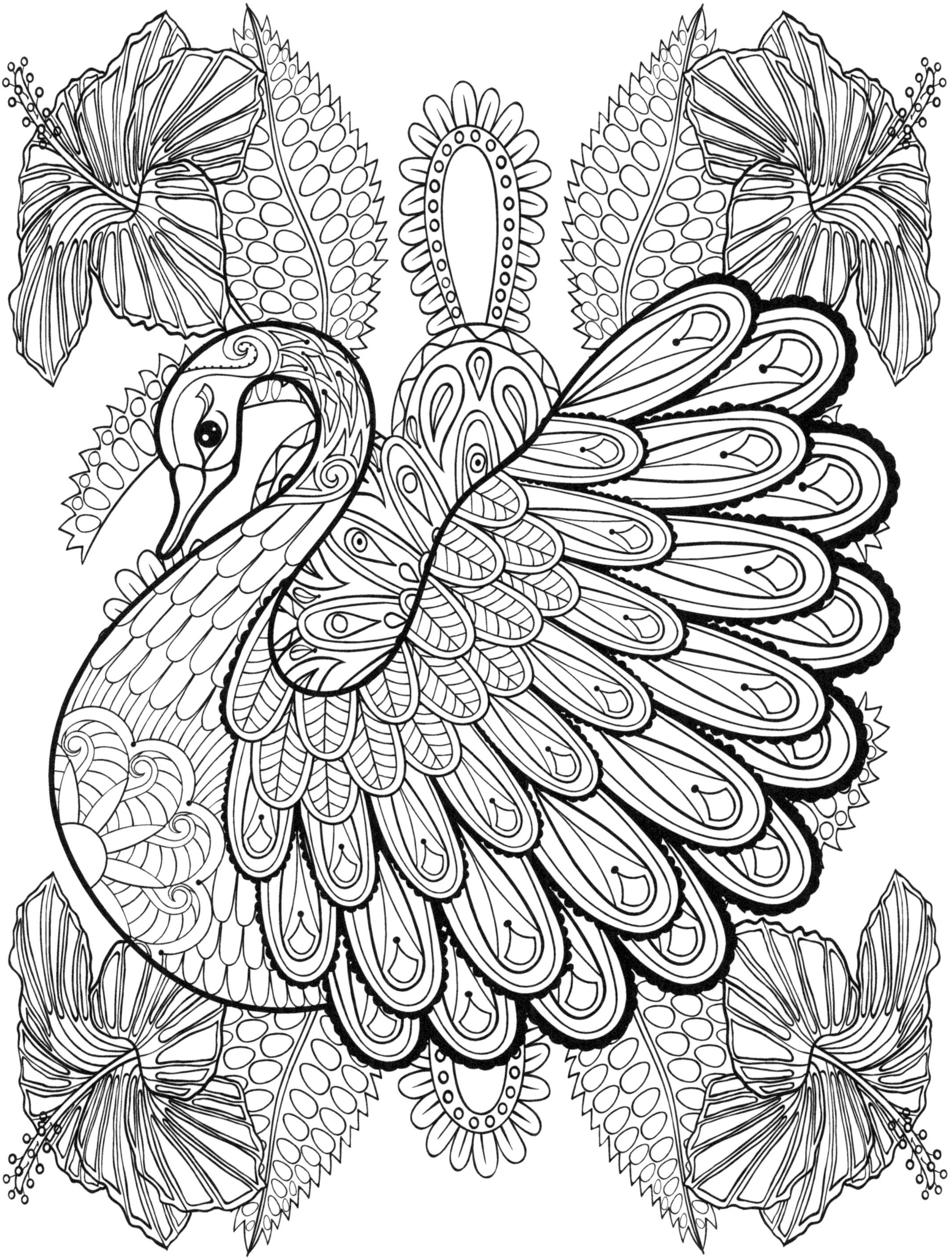

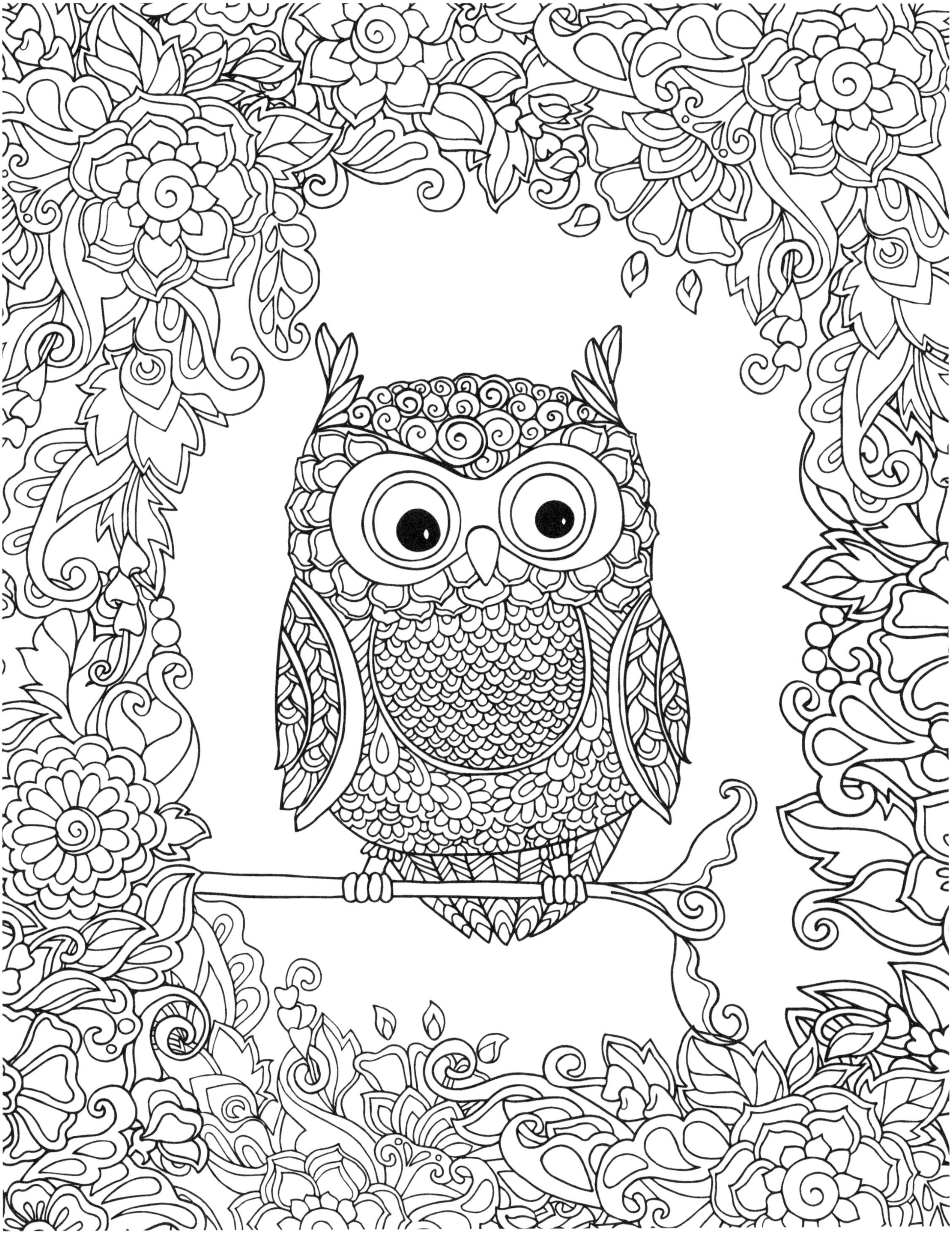

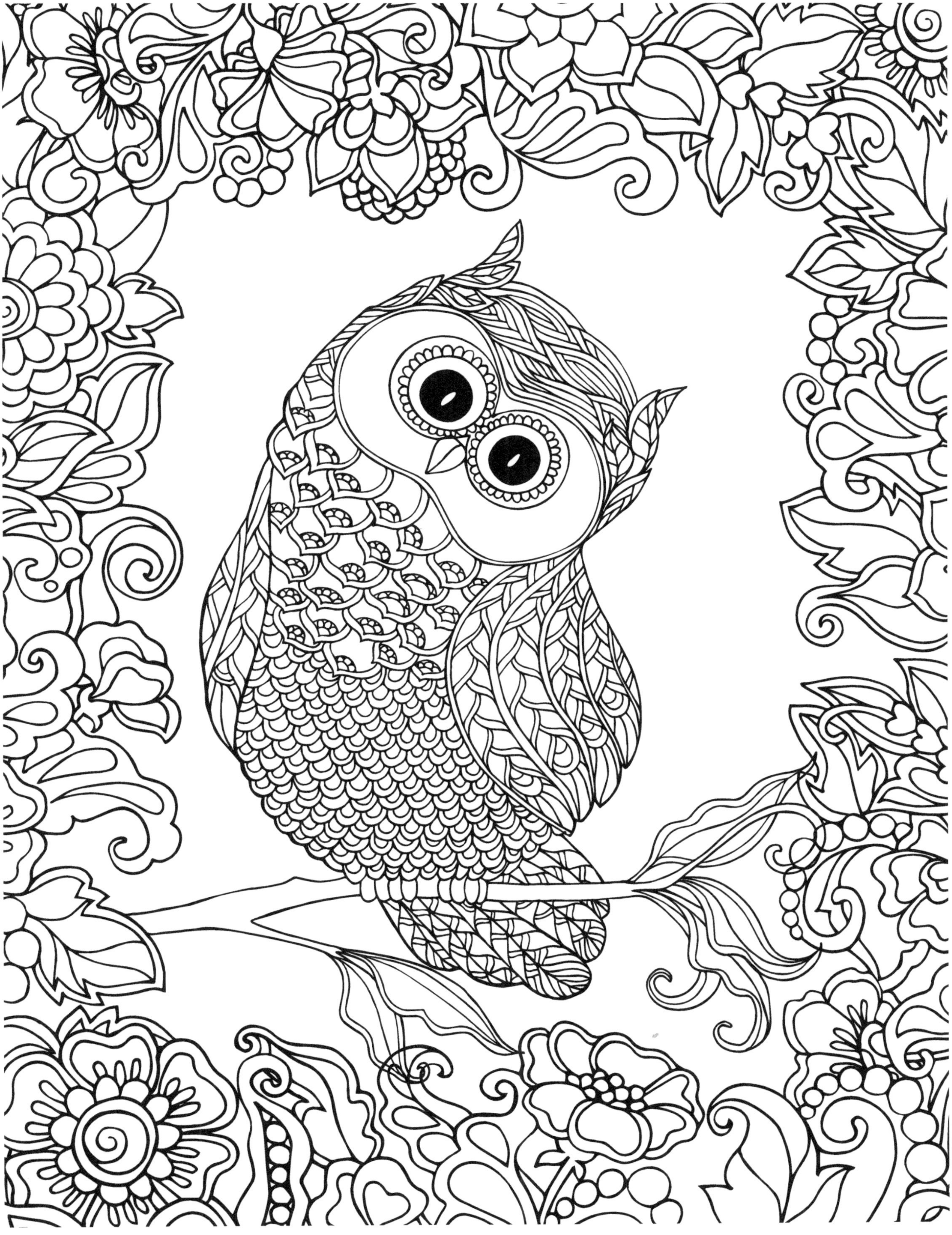

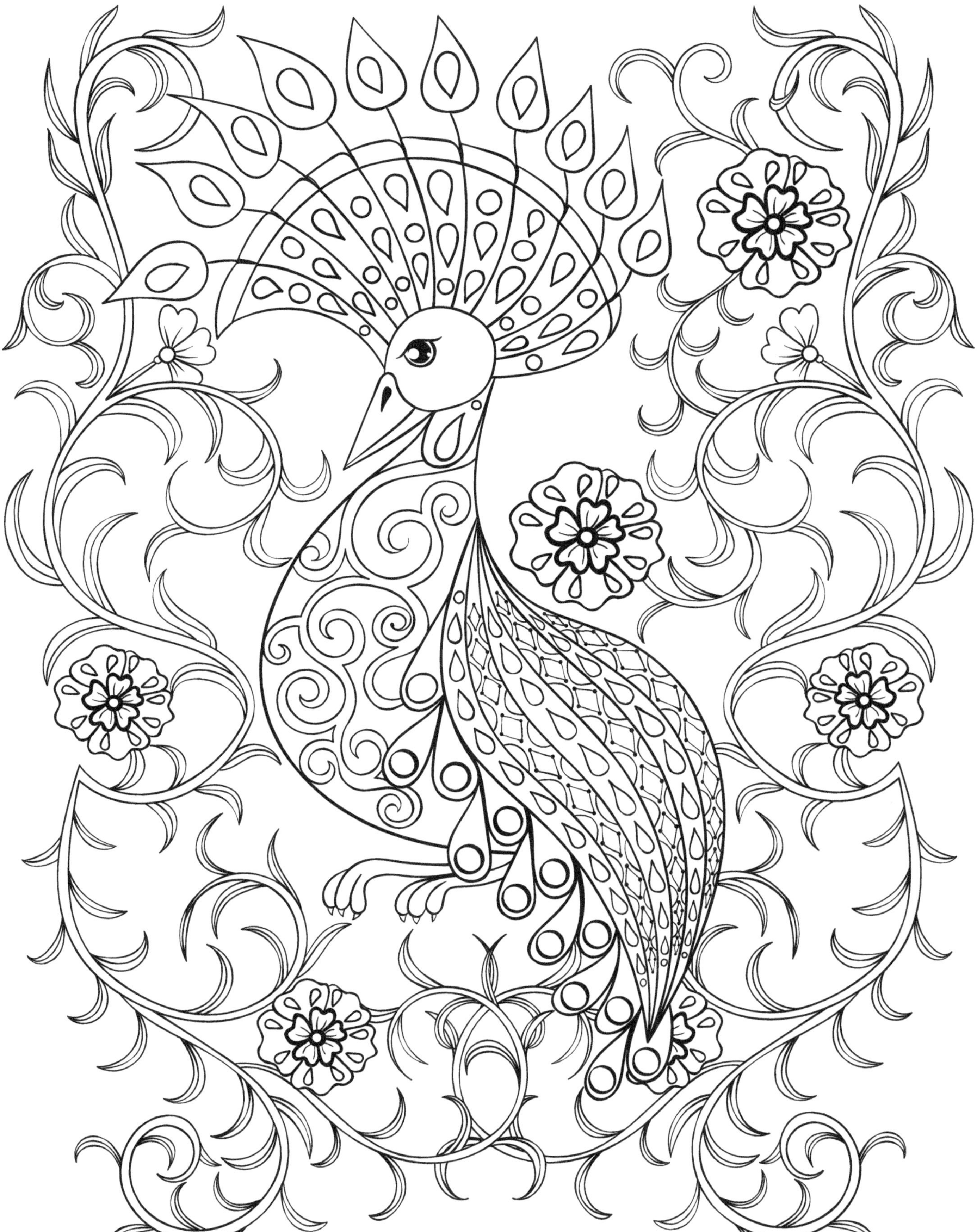

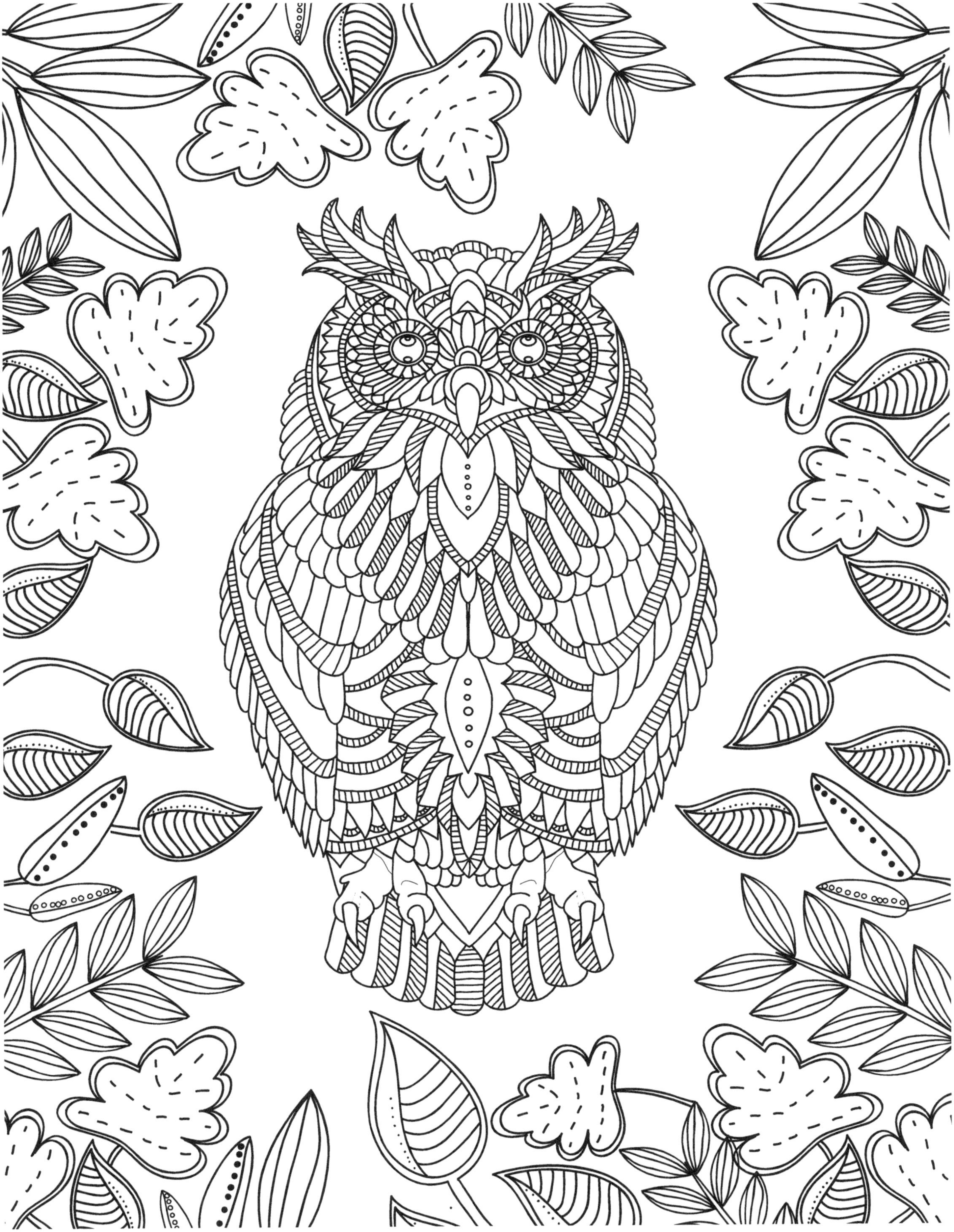

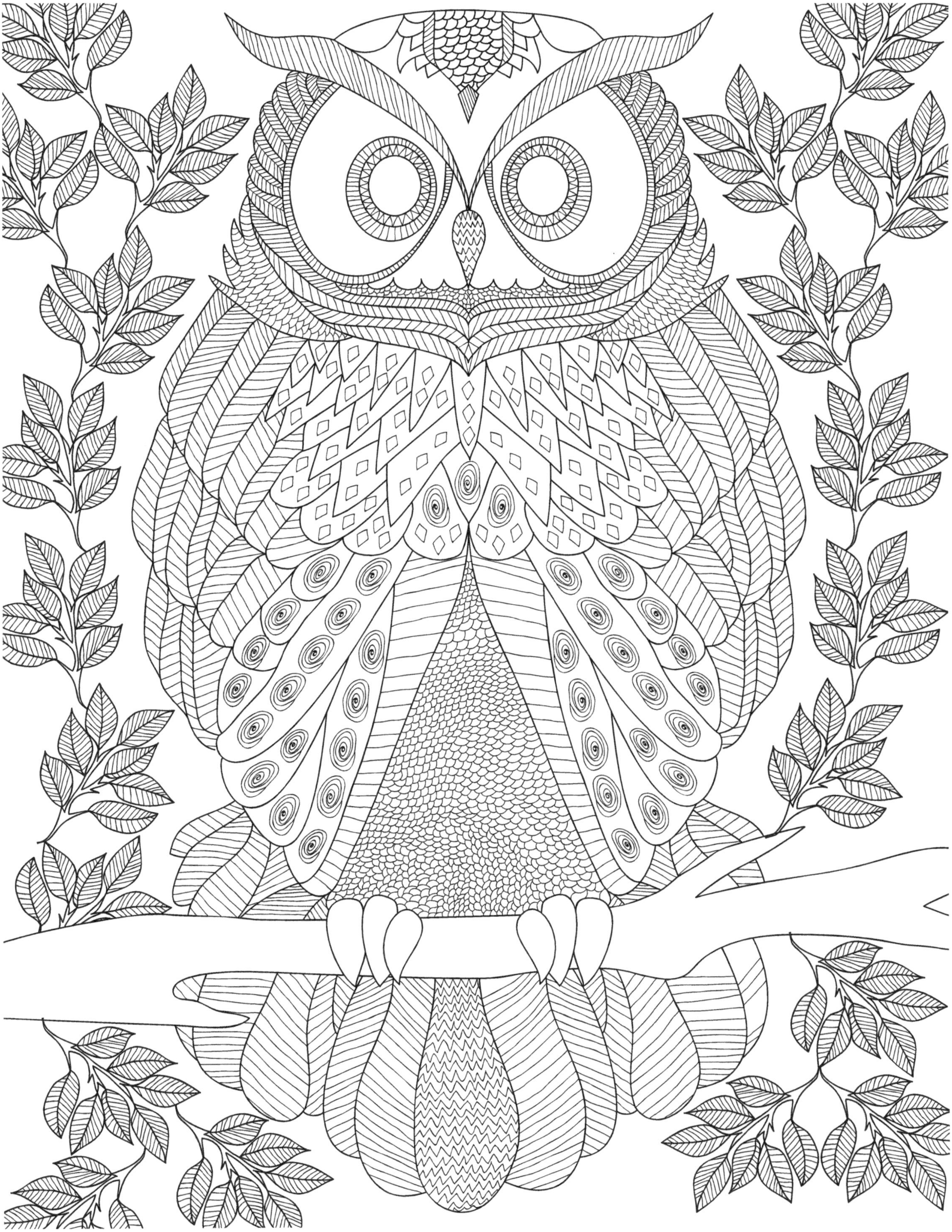

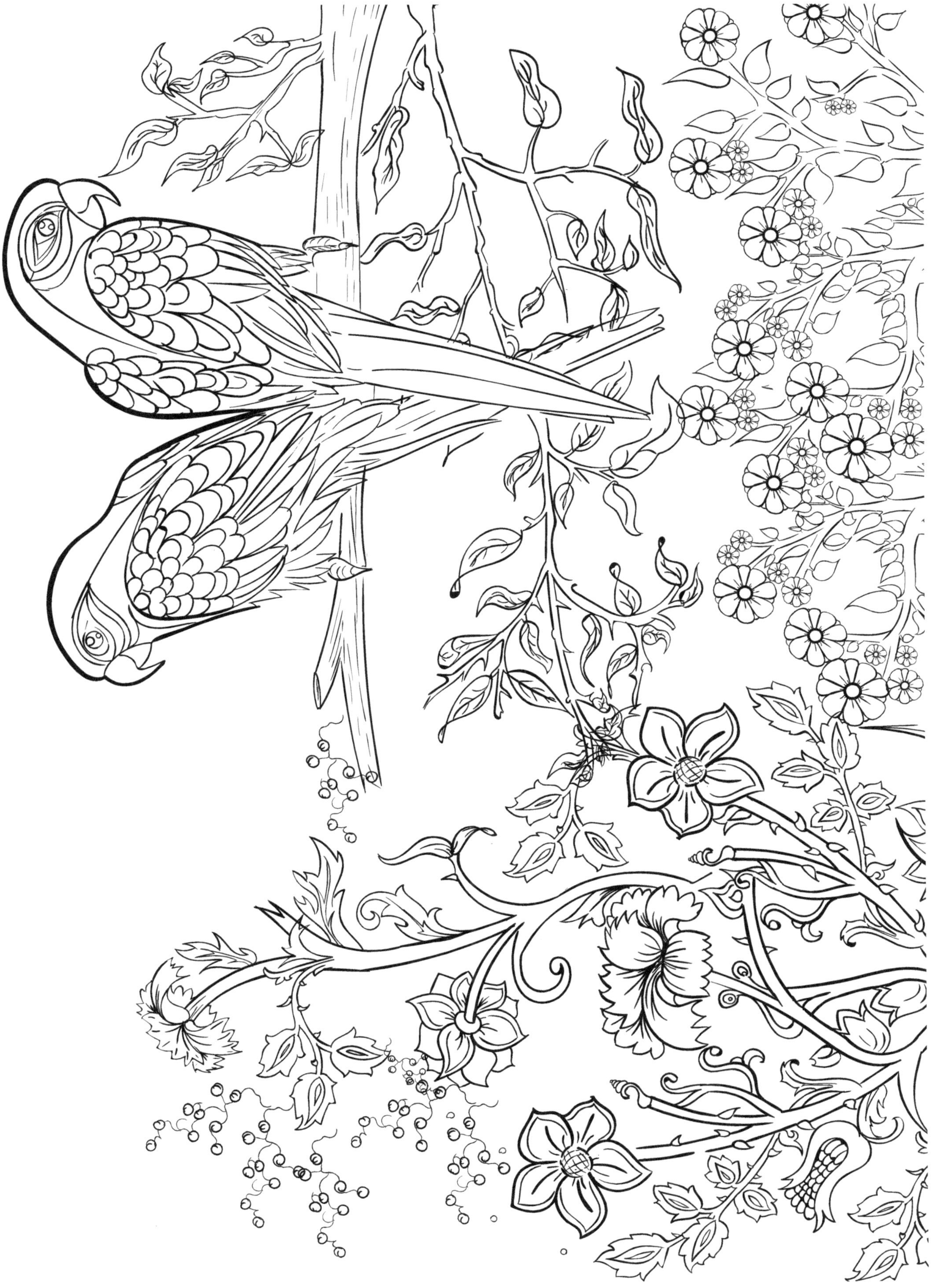

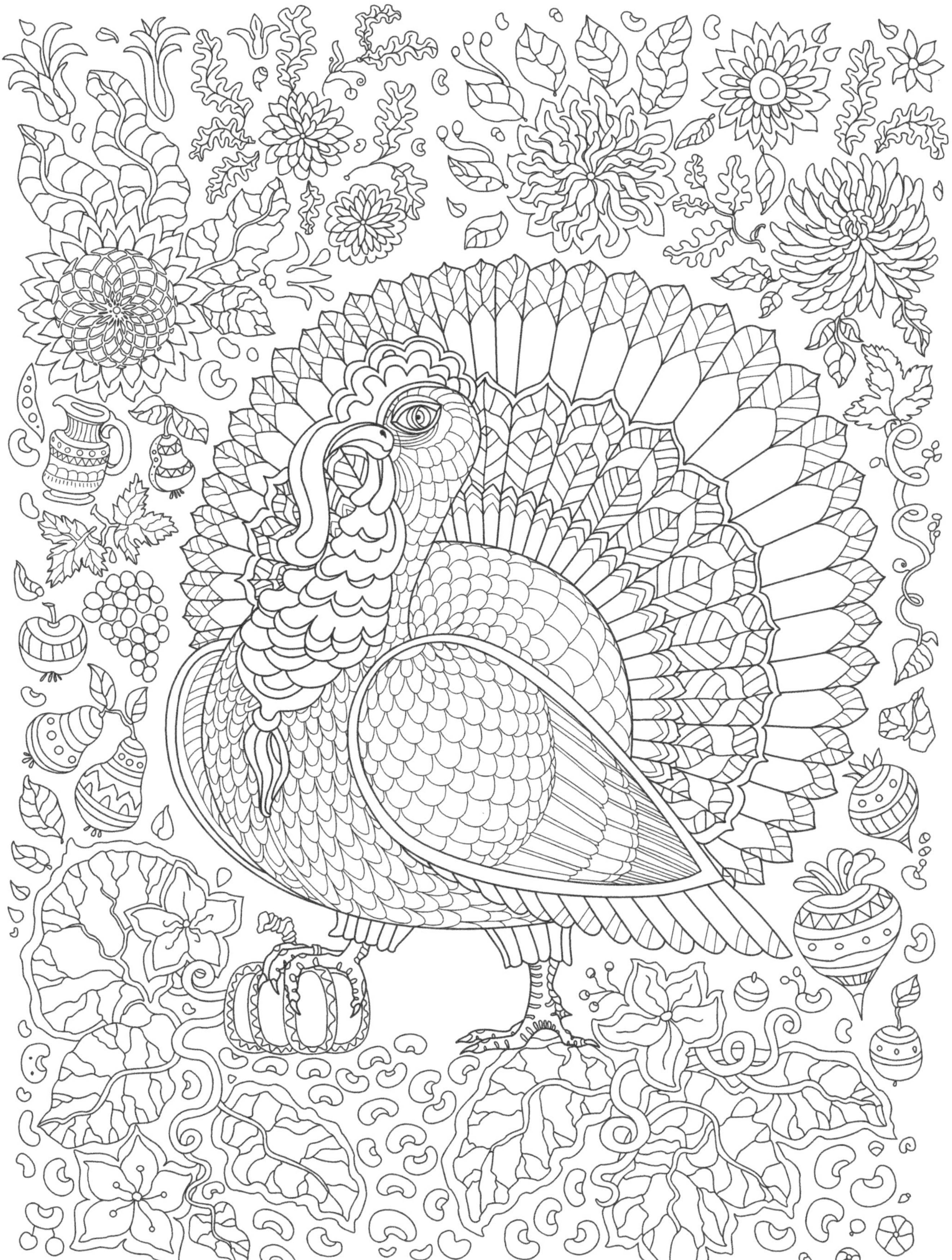

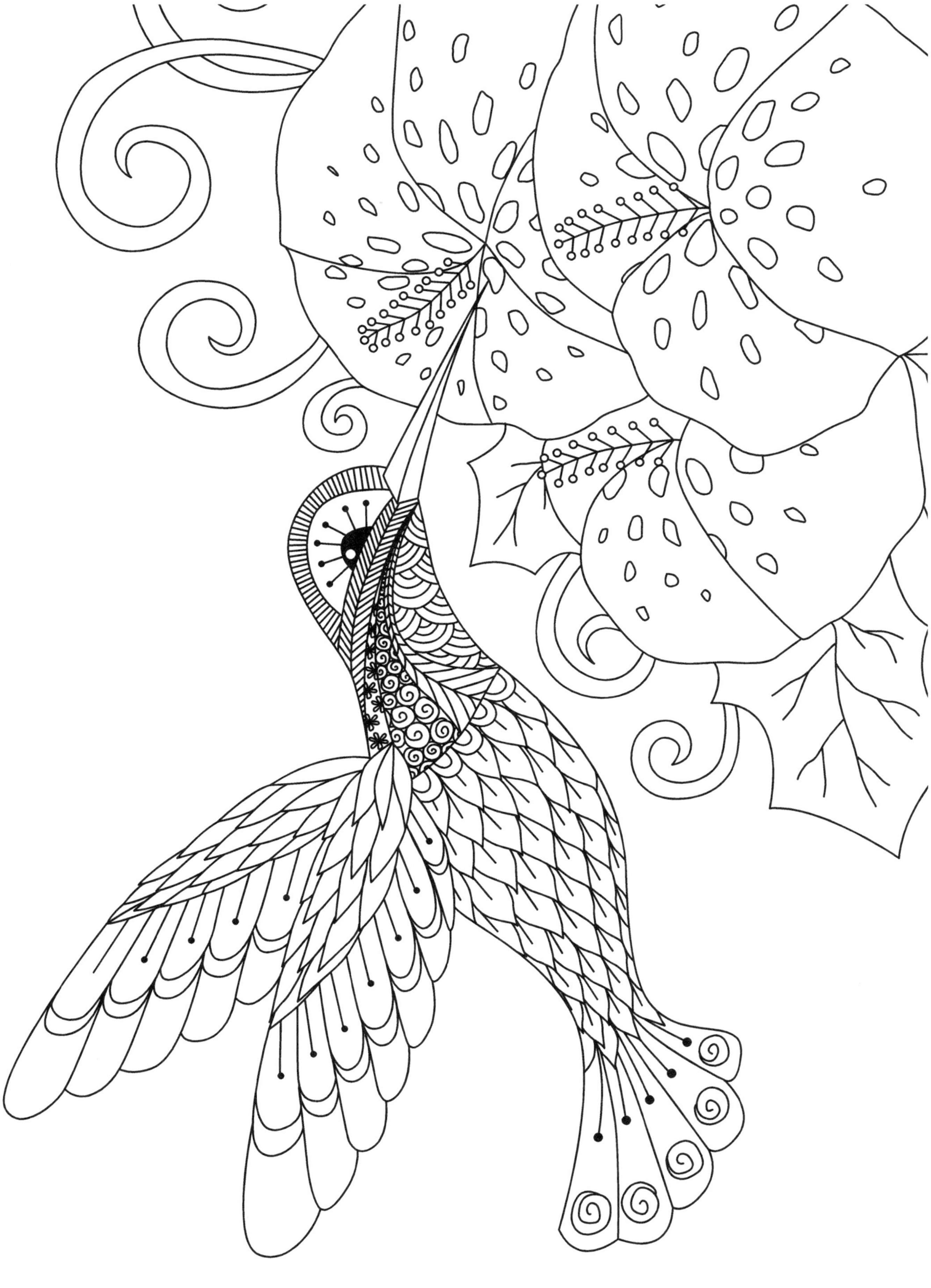

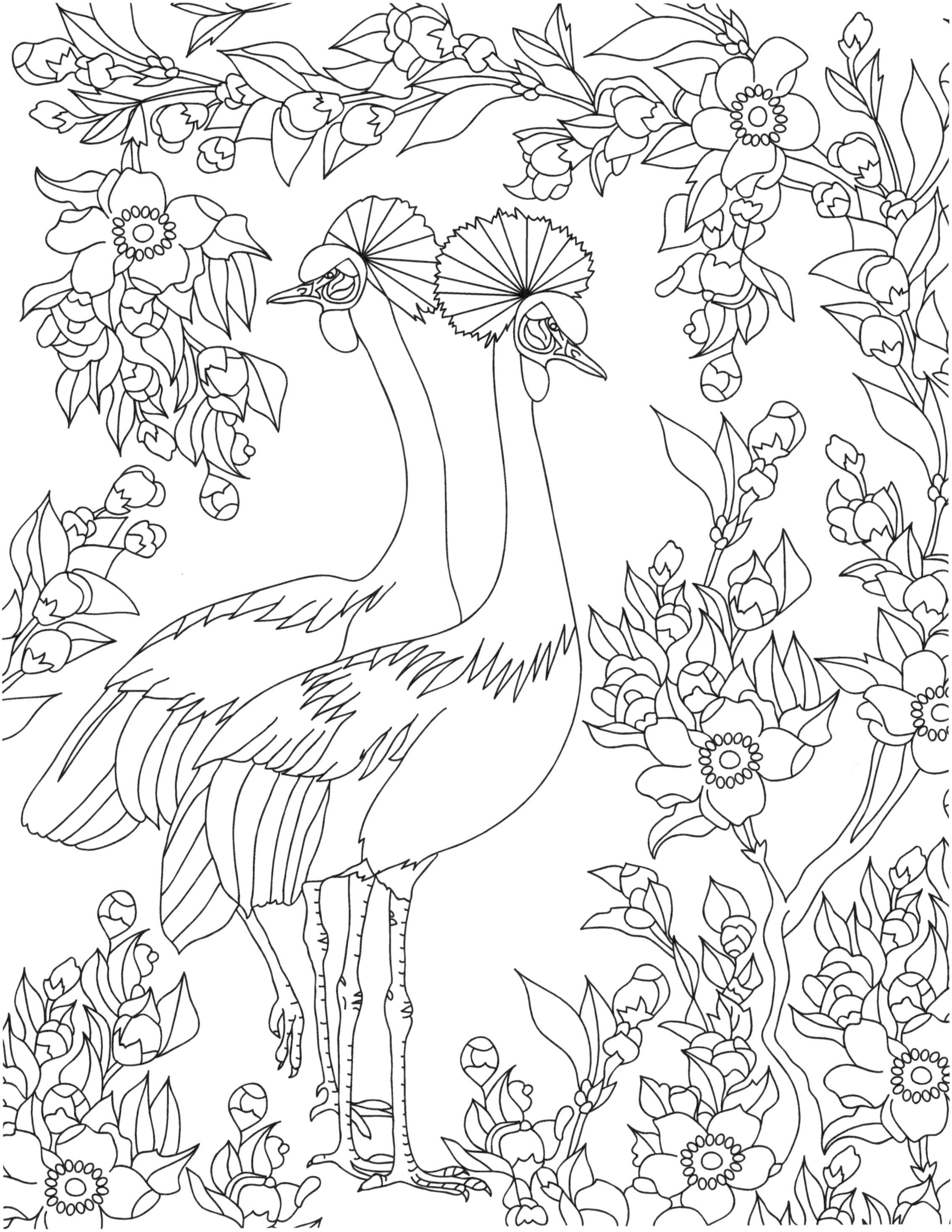

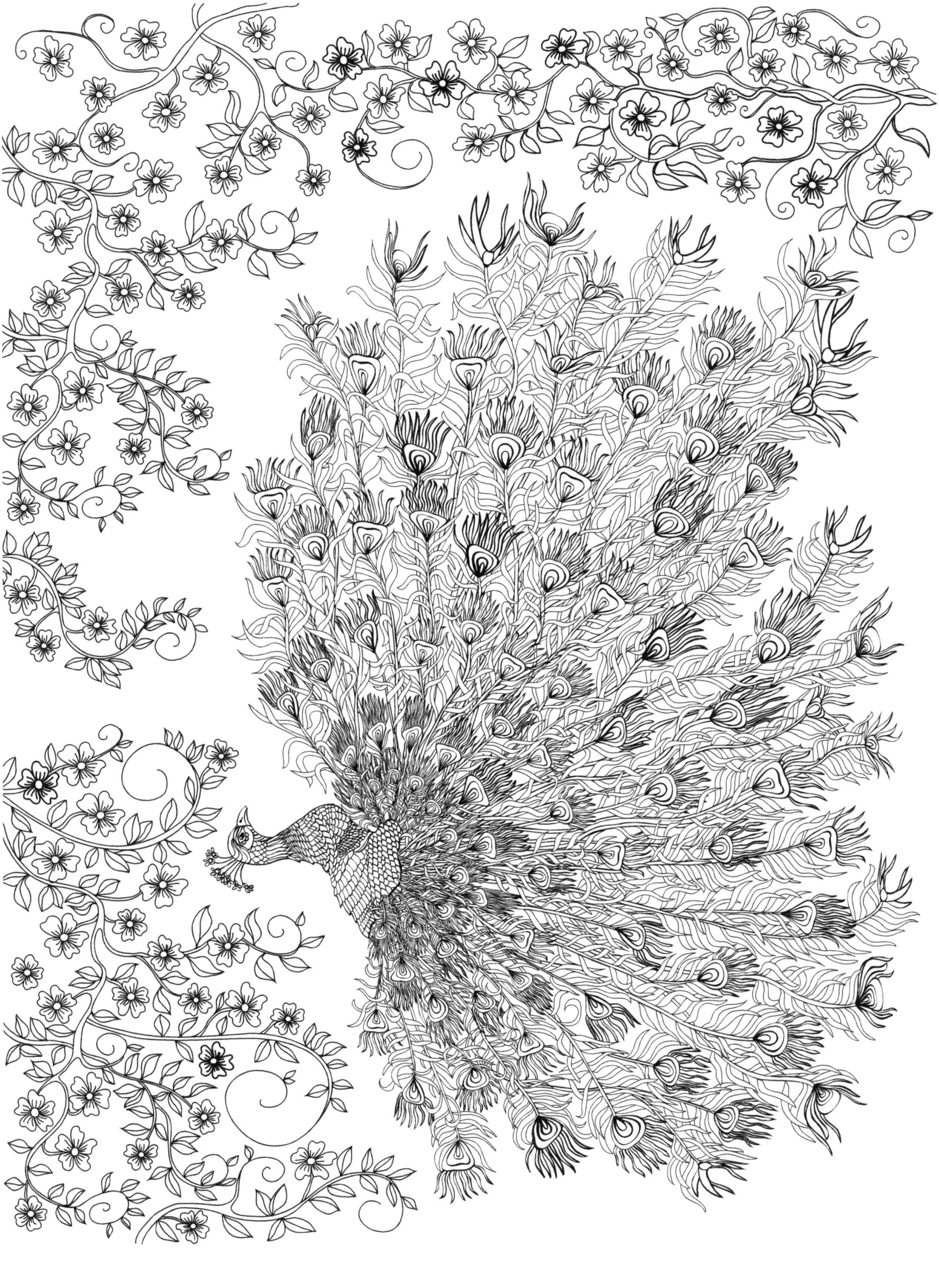

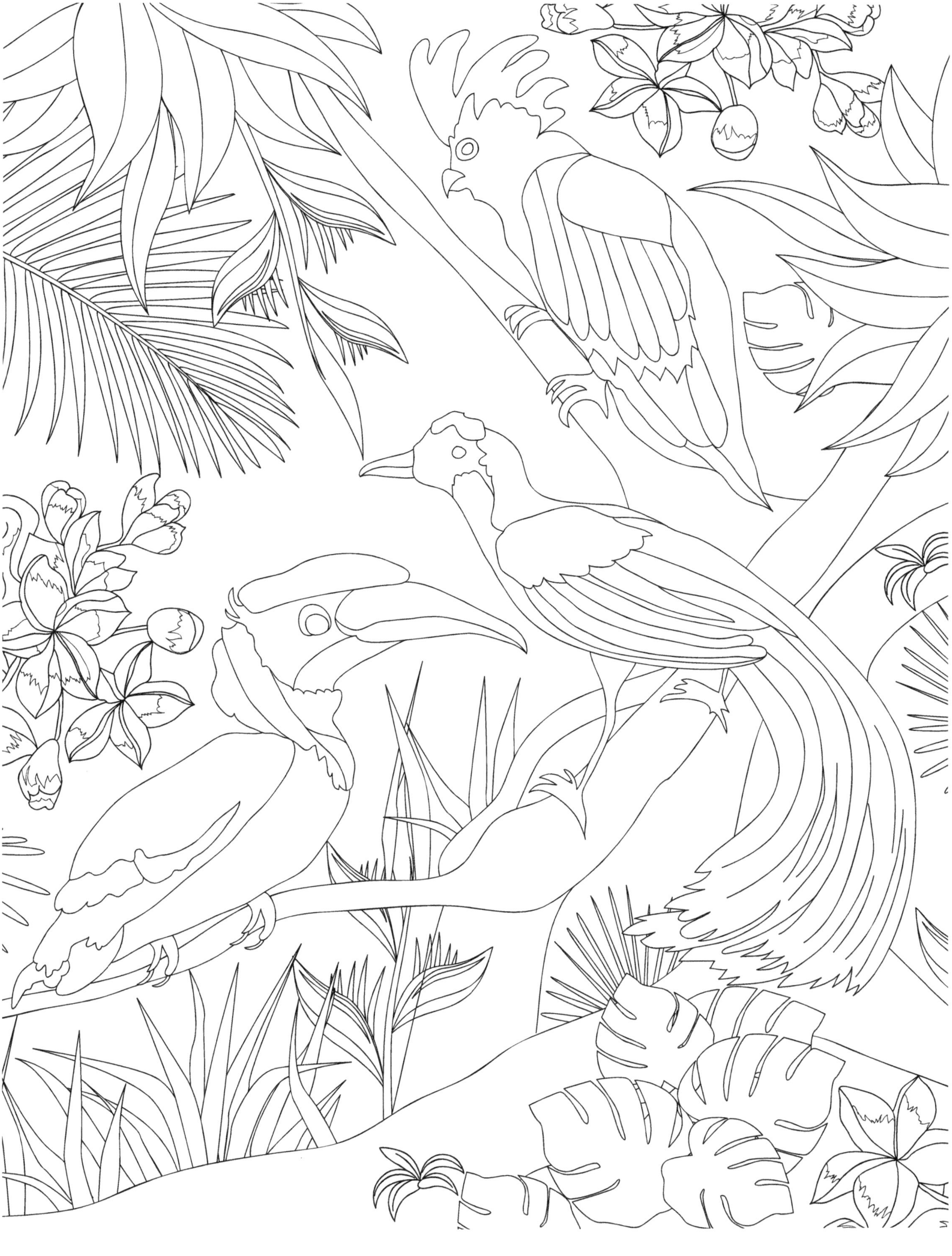

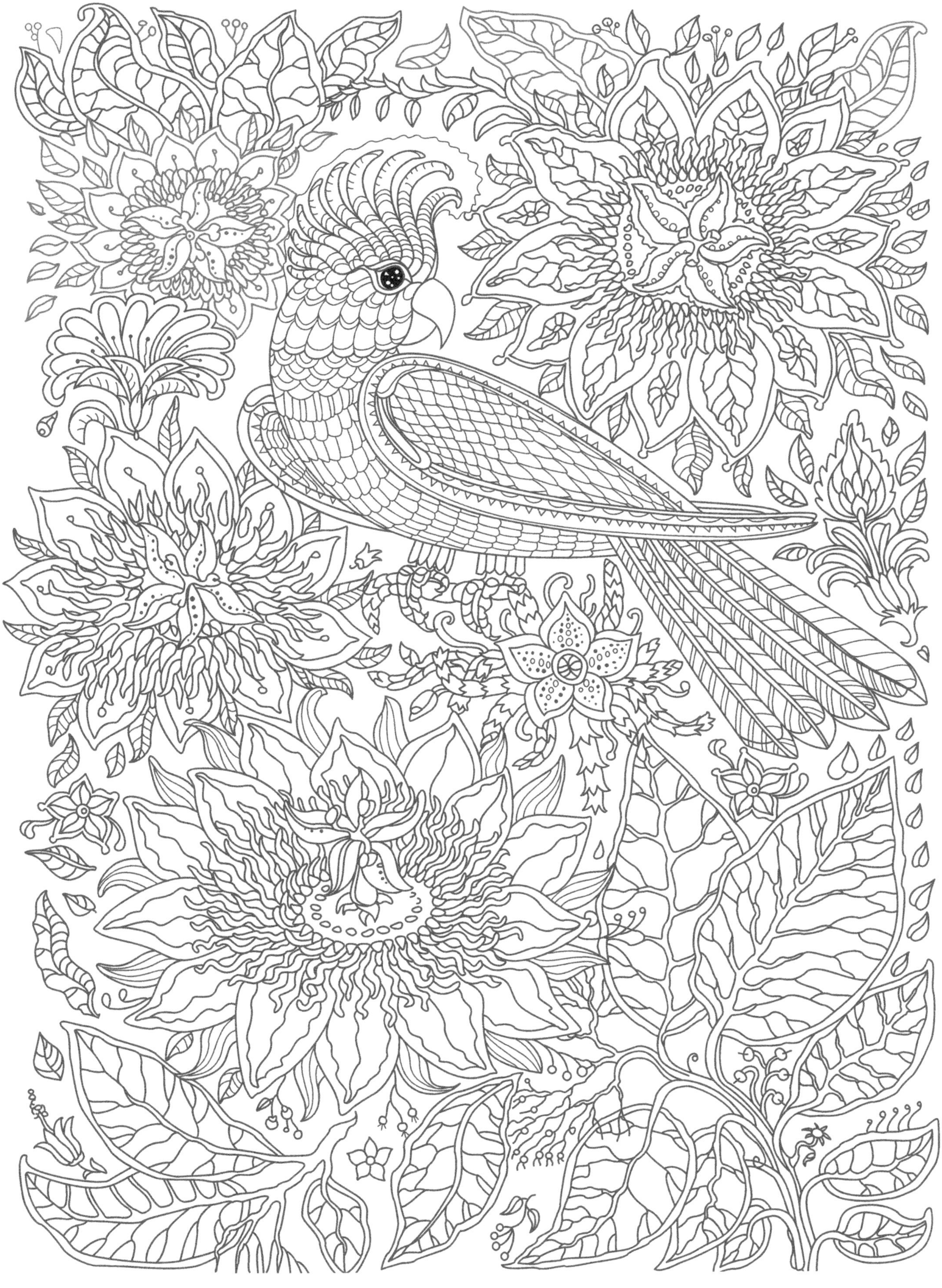

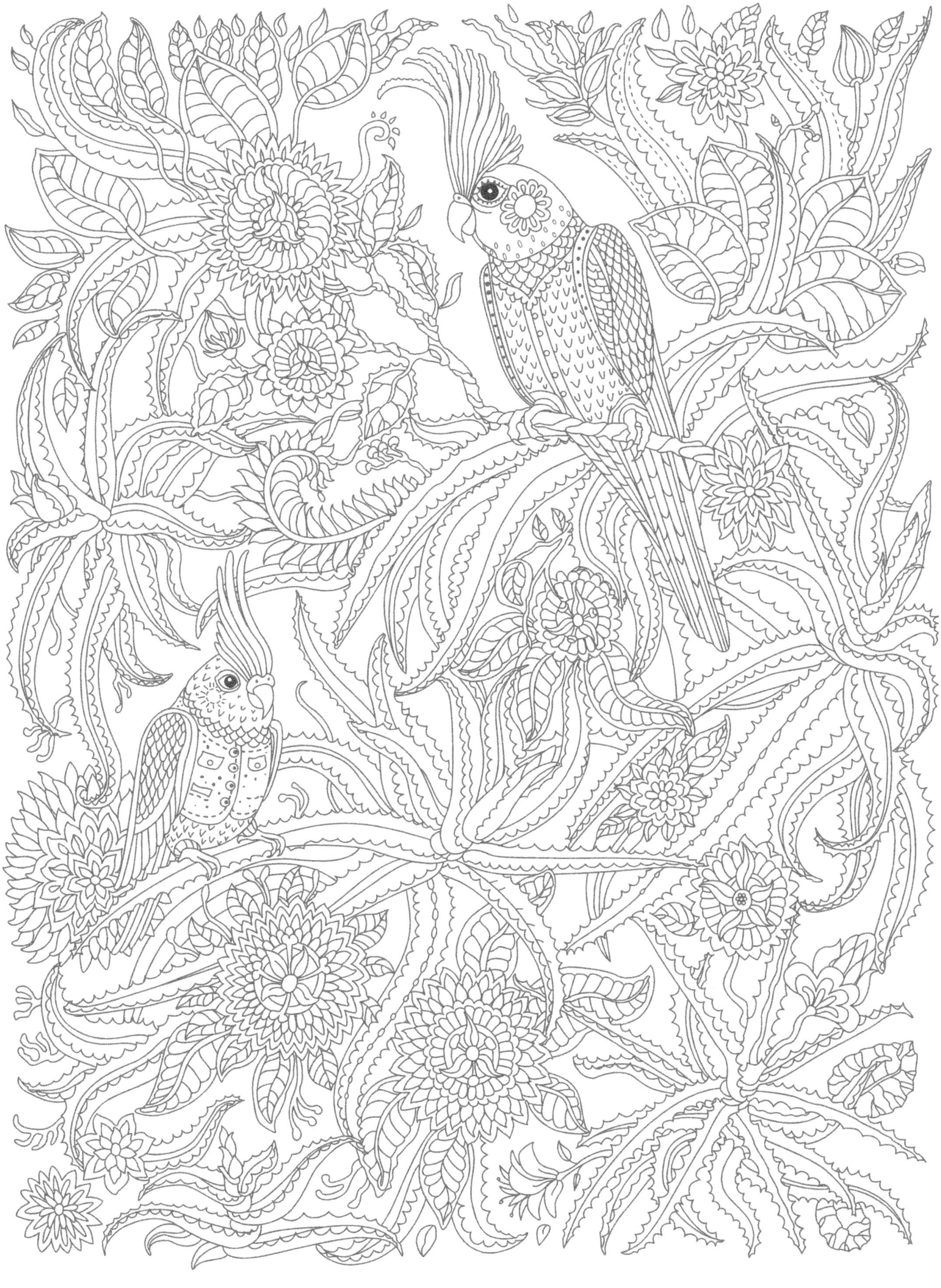

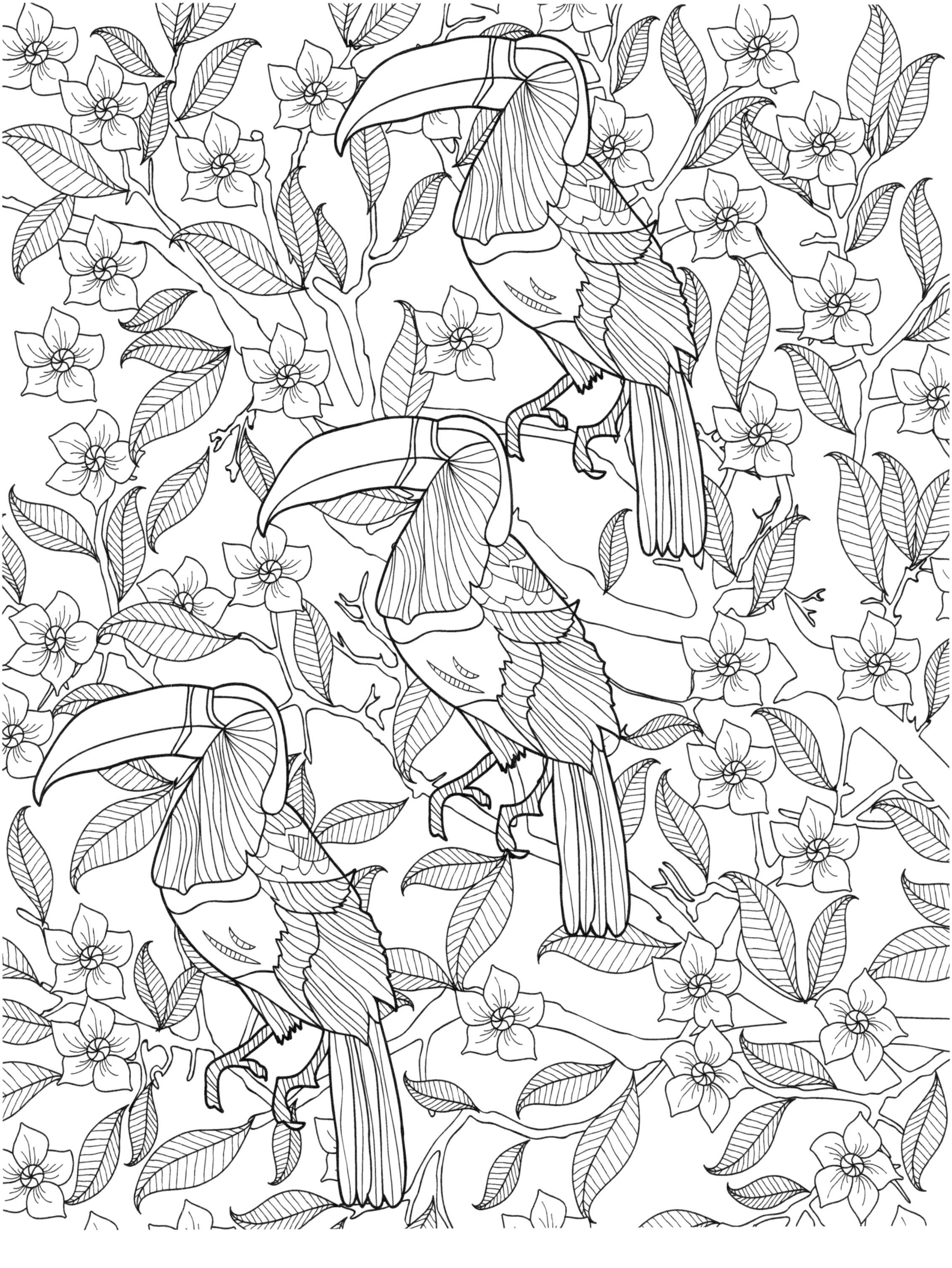

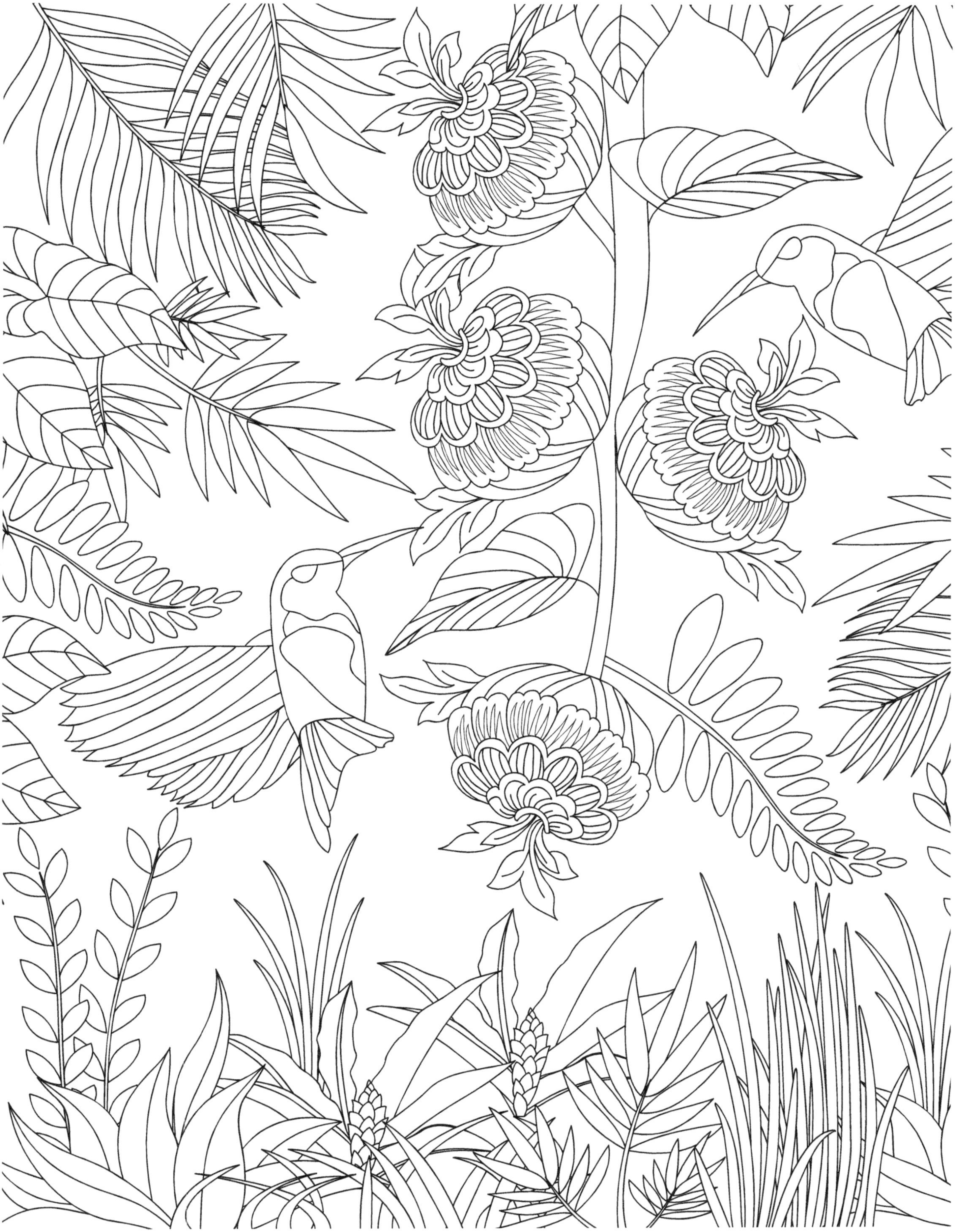

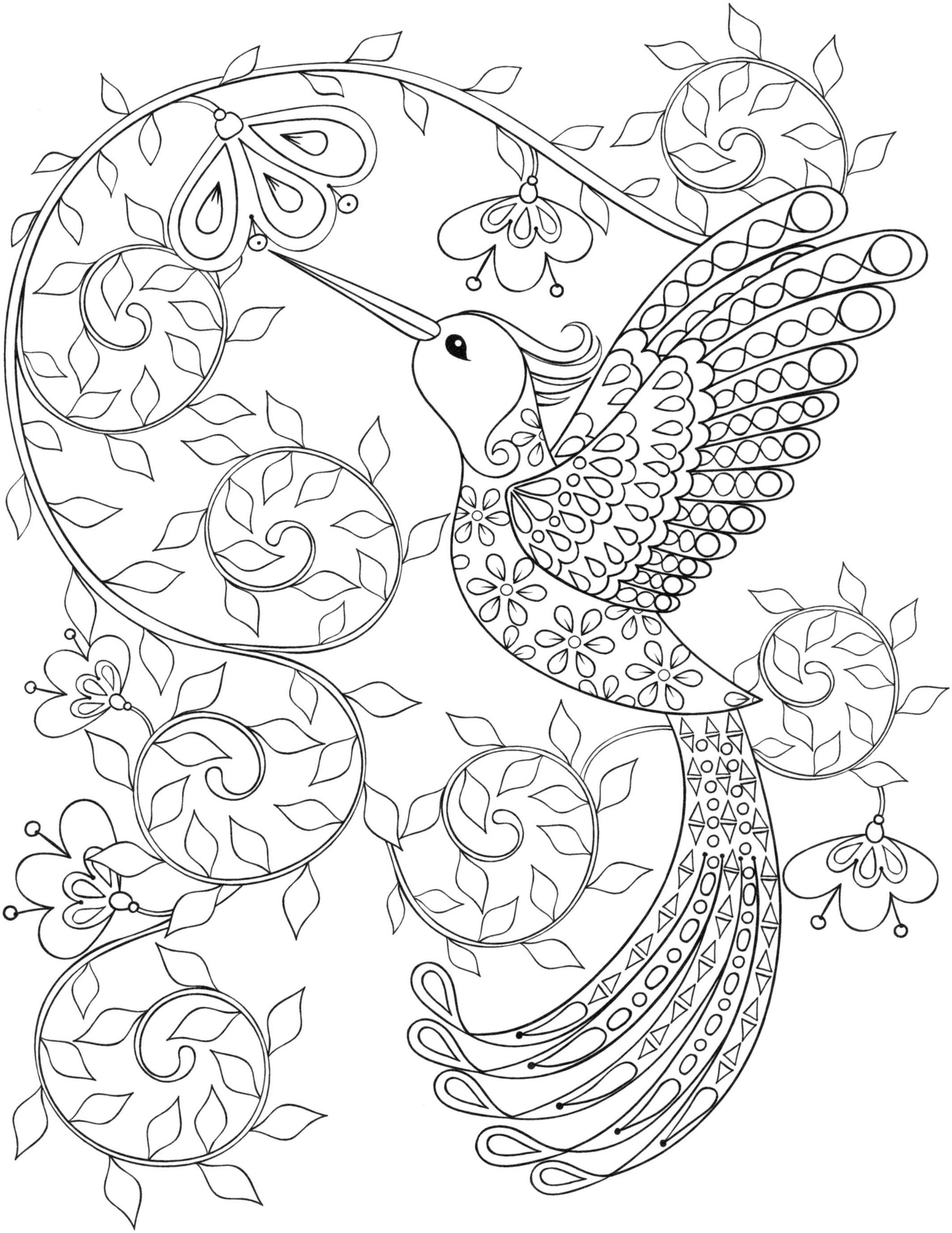

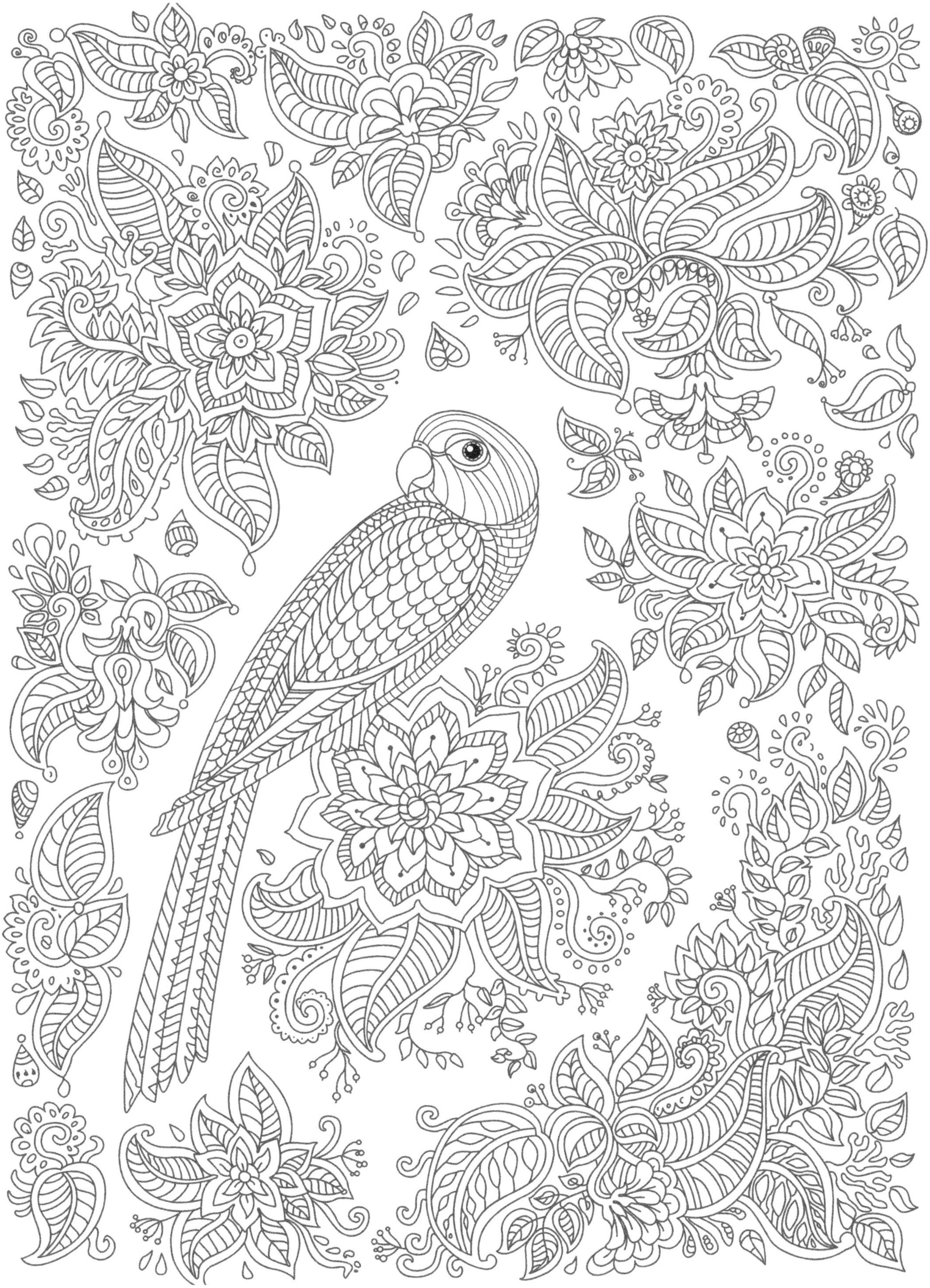

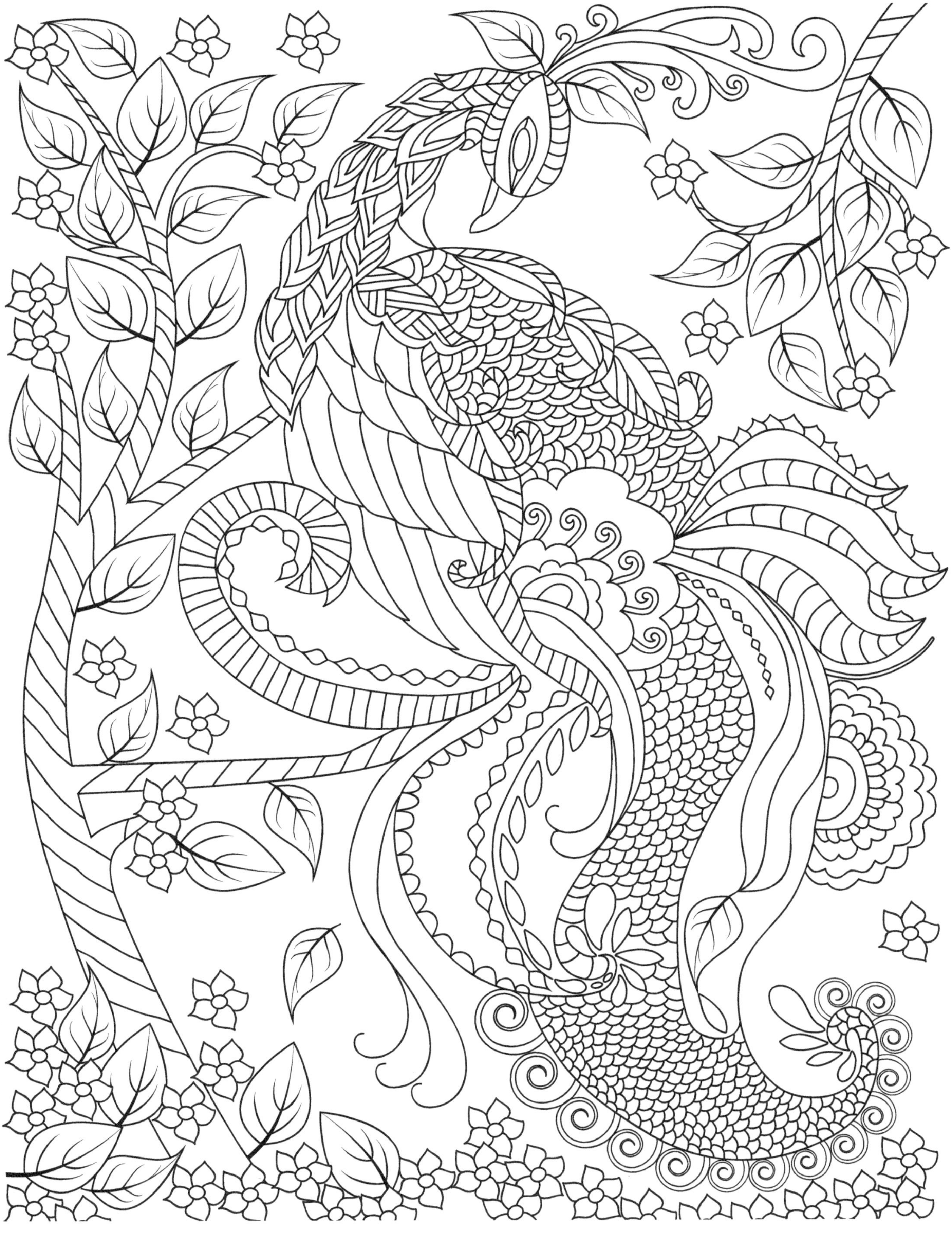

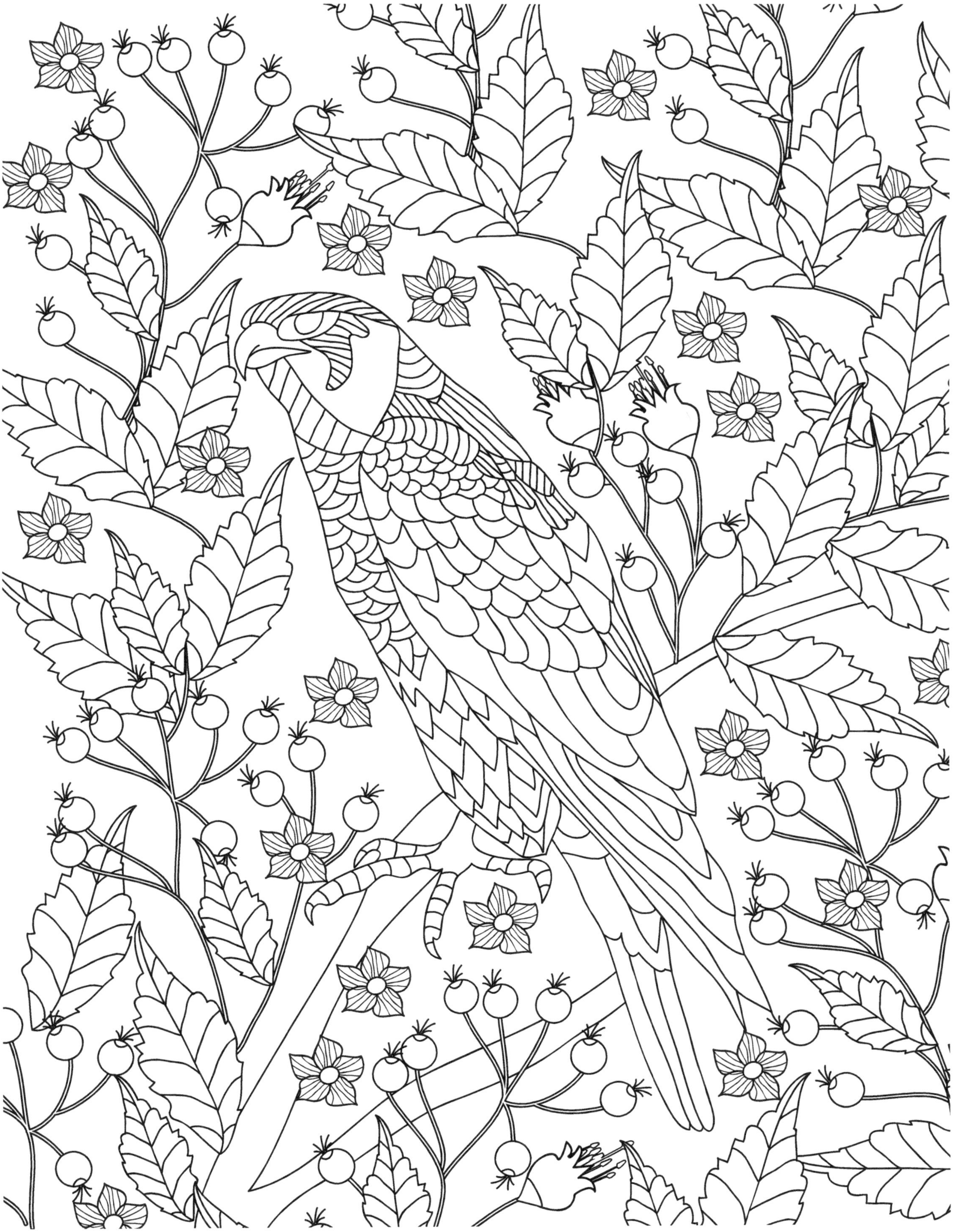

www.ingramcontent.com/pod-product-compliance
Lightning Source LLC
Chambersburg PA
CBHW080539190526
45169CB00007B/2555
*9781530682300*